# THE SAVING GRACE OF GOD

By Cheyenne Thomas

THE SAVING GRACE OF GOD

# DEDICATION

This book is dedicated to my wife, Joanne (also known as Momma Joe, the mother of our children); to my children, Takiyah, LaTesha, Nehemiah, and Dinah; and to my grandchildren. Each of you has inspired me in writing this and my other books. I am also grateful to my siblings, Nancy, Dianne, Elgotoe, Carlos, Dylane, Wanda, and Aurora, some of whom have gone home to be with the Lord; your support has been a blessing and an inspiration. To my mother and grandmother, who both raised me, I owe who I am today. Last but not least, to my Heavenly Father: the Almighty God, Jesus Christ (His beloved and only begotten Son), and the Holy Spirit. All glory, honor, and praise belong to you. Thank You for the wisdom, knowledge, understanding, and revelations you have shared with me through Your Word.

THE SAVING GRACE OF GOD

# CONTENTS

# THE SAVING GRACE OF GOD

# ACKNOWLEDGMENTS

I would like to express my sincere gratitude to the three most important beings in my life. First, thank you, Lord Jesus Christ, for completing the task of redeeming my soul. Second, I give thank to the His Heavenly Father, the Almighty God, for sending His Son to redeem us, offering His life on the Cross at Calvary. Third, we are grateful to the Holy Spirit, who guides and leads us, reminding us of Jesus' words. I am immensely grateful for the gift of Grace bestowed upon me, a gift I do not deserve and cannot earn. In your great love, compassion, and mercy, you have given me eternal life through Jesus Christ. Words cannot express the gratitude you deserve for what you have done for me, yet with all my heart and soul, I thank you.

My deepest gratitude goes to my wife, Joanne Thomas, and our children: Takiyah Nickerson, LaTesha C. Thomas, Nehemiah A. Thomas, and Dinah J. Thomas, for their encouragement and support throughout this writing journey. Special thanks to my grandchildren, whose joy and love inspire me.

To my siblings: Nancy Thomas, Dianne Thomas, Elgotoe Thomas, Carlos Simms, Dylane Kelly, Wanda Kate, and Aurora Thomas, along with his wife, Sandra Thomas. I offer my sincere thanks. Your support and encouragement have been invaluable. Also, thank you for helping me proofread my work.

I wish to extend my heartfelt gratitude to my pastor, Dr. Joseph M. Ripley Sr. I am deeply thankful for his inspirational leadership, his unwavering example as a beacon of light, and his exemplary life as a faithful child of God. The wisdom, knowledge, understanding, and revelation of God's Word, imparted through his ministry, have been a profound blessing to me. I give thanks to God for granting me the privilege of partaking in and sharing these spiritual gifts.

To the members of The Body of Christ Church International USA, my Church Family, I am thankful for your warm smiles, kindness, fellowship, and love. You have been a blessing in my life, encouraging me throughout this process.

Finally, I would like to express my sincere gratitude to Ambassador Everett Robinson for his kindness, inspiration, and unwavering friendship. His exposition of New Testament doctrine, faithfully transmitted in accordance with the teaching of the biblical apostles, has proven of great benefit to the community of believers. These teachings are of inestimable value to the Body of Christ.

THE SAVING GRACE OF GOD

# INTRODUCTION

Ʒrom the moment of Adam's disobedience and the fall of man, the stain of sin began to rule over humanity. This book asserts as its central thesis: God's saving grace, given through His only begotten Son, Jesus Christ, is essential and available for the redemption and transformation of all humanity. Therefore, at the appointed time, God sent His Word, His only begotten Son, into the world to redeem and save humanity.

This book delves into the profound concept of God's saving grace, exploring its origins and significance in the lives of individuals. It aims to illuminate the essence of this grace, clarifying who it is intended for and the transformative impact it has on humanity. Understanding God's saving grace is crucial for mankind, as it reveals the depth of divine love and the purpose it serves in our lives. Furthermore, the book emphasizes that this extraordinary grace is accessible to all, providing guidance on how individuals can embrace and receive it in their own journeys through life.

As a disciple of Jesus Christ and a child of the living God, I have, throughout my life, encountered many wondrous experiences, some so profound that words fail to fully capture their depth, and others so mysterious that they defy human explanation. Yet, each of these moments has been an immeasurable blessing, a testament to the grace and goodness of God. I would now pose a question to you: Have you ever received or experienced something so extraordinary that it could not be explained? Perhaps you have been given something you could neither afford nor merit, a gift entirely unearned. Let me speak to you of a matter of supreme and profound importance, one that bears eternal significance and terrible consequences for all humanity if not received: the subject of *Grace,* specifically, *The Saving Grace of God.* It is my desire that every reader not only comprehends the definition of grace but also grasps its value, necessity, and transformative power. In the life of the believer, there is no concept more essential to understand and receive.

Within the Church, the word "Grace" is spoken often, in sermons, hymns, and everyday conversation, because it is woven throughout the fabric of Holy Scripture. Yet frequent mention does not always equal deep understanding. Ask yourself, do I truly know the value, the purpose, the meaning, and the power behind the word *grace*? Therefore, I invite you to pause and reflect personally: *What does grace mean to me as a follower of Christ? Do I truly know the value and purpose of grace and the power it possess? Have I come to understand its full significance? Can I rightly articulate and comprehend what Scripture reveals as this Amazing Grace of God?*

In this book, *The Saving Grace of God,* I will seek to unfold the biblical meaning of grace, as revealed in the Word of God, and to explain why it is indispensable to the salvation and sanctification of humanity. Along the way, I will share insights and illumination which I believe the Lord Jesus Christ, through the Holy Spirit, has granted to me. My aim is to guide you toward a clearer understanding of foundational questions and themes, including: "What is grace?" "Grace through Jesus Christ," "What was Jesus' purpose in coming?" "The saving grace of God "and" How can one receive God's amazing grace?"

As in my other writings, I wish to make a parenthetical statement at the outset: Certain truths I present herein, I hold to be revelation knowledge imparted by the Lord Jesus Christ through The Holy Spirit. These insights may not be directly provable by specific chapter and verse, apart from the reminder of John 21:25 that not all of Christ's works and sayings are recorded in Scripture, but on the other hand neither can anyone disprove them as well because I believe they were given to me by the Lord.

As we seek to understand what God's saving grace is and why mankind stands in desperate need of it, I urge you to pray earnestly for the Lord to grant you personal revelation. Keep your Bible at hand. Consult reputable concordances such as Strong's Exhaustive Concordance, the CSB Concordance, or Young's Analytical Concordance, many of which are available online. Do not rely solely on my words; examine the Scriptures and pursue diligent studies, for in doing so, you will gain a deeper, richer, and more personal grasp of God's truth or the truth of God's Word.

It is my prayer that the Lord would enlighten the eyes of your heart and understanding, bestowing wisdom and discernment, and leading you into a deeper knowledge of His saving grace. May the illumination of God's Word inspire a more faithful walk with Him, as a devoted disciple of Jesus Christ and a beloved child of God.

As we journey through these pages, we will seek to grasp the true depth of God's amazing grace, His saving grace, and discover why it is far more than just a good idea. It is the very heartbeat of God's love for us (all of humanity).

⟨ CHAPTER 1 ⟩

# WHAT IS GRACE

## The Testimony of Grace

𝐼n the vast tapestry of theological discourse, few concepts are as crucial and transformative as the notion of grace. The very essence of grace is woven into the fabric of divine interaction with humanity, serving as a cornerstone of spiritual understanding and religious practice. (Grace | Definition, Description, Christianity, & Beliefs, n.d.) To comprehend the origins of saving grace, one must delve into its multifaceted nature, exploring its manifestations as undeserved kindness, daily sustenance, forgiveness, and strength in weakness. These elements are not merely abstract ideas but are deeply embedded in the lived experiences and spiritual journeys of countless individuals throughout history.

But, before we embark any further upon this theological exploration of divine grace, I desire to share a personal testimony of its reality in my own life. On various occasions, while driving for my vocation, I have been suddenly overcome with a joy so profound and a peace so deep that no human language can fully articulate it. In such moments, there is an unshakable assurance in my soul, a holy certainty that God is real, that He is infinitely holy, and that His love surpasses all human comprehension. This joy is not the fruit of my own merit or spiritual effort; it is a gracious gift from God, a manifestation of His unmerited favor toward me.

I am convinced that I am not the only recipient of

such divine visitations, for our God is too great to confine such revelations to one soul alone. Rather, He delights to make Himself known to His people, granting them blessed assurance that He alone is God and there is none besides Him. Through the atoning work of His Son, Jesus Christ, the living God now dwells within me. (Bible Verses about Holy Spirit, Indwelling of, n.d.) Though my eyes have not yet seen Him, my faith assures me of His reality, and my life in Christ enables me to commune with Him in a manner pleasing to His heart.

To all who have tasted this joy, let us together lift our voices in praise to the Giver of every good and perfect gift. To those who have not, my prayer is that the Lord would graciously open your heart to receive the blessed assurance of His presence, that you too might know Him as the Almighty God. Whether the day be radiant with sunlight or shrouded in gloom, His mercy remains. I cannot attribute this joy to my faith alone nor to any work of my own, but solely to the grace, mercy, and love of God, lavished upon me though I am undeserving. Truly, Christ has done this for me. Hallelujah!

There are times when I perceive the world through what I call "the eyes of the inner man." In such moments, I behold the beauty of God's creation and see His handiwork displayed in all that He has made. Yet when my attention returns to the affairs of this world, I see the brokenness of humanity, men and women living without knowledge of God, acting without remorse, compassion, or love, as though driven by a spirit of darkness. I know that such lives are not governed by the Spirit of God, but by the fallen systems of this world under the influence of the powers of evil; Satan and his demons. (Monnig & S, 2019)

Oh, that God would open their spiritual eyes to perceive the truth of His Word and the grace and mercy He has freely given!

## The Essence of Grace

Grace, in its most extensive and elemental form, is a concept that transcends the boundaries of human understanding, touching the very core of spiritual and existential inquiry. It is an unearned, unmerited favor that flows from the divine, an expression of love that is neither conditional nor transactional. To grasp the essence of grace is to embark on a journey that explores the depths of compassion, forgiveness, and benevolence, attributes that are often ascribed to The Power of God. In this part of the chapter, we will delve into the multifaceted nature of grace, examining its various types, meanings, and the joy it brings to those who embrace it. At its core, grace is the antithesis of the merit-based systems that govern much of human society. It is not something that can be earned through deeds or accomplishments but is rather a gift bestowed freely and generously. This concept of grace challenges the conventional wisdom that rewards are always a direct result of effort and merit. In theological terms, grace is often described as the divine influence that operates in individuals to regenerate and sanctify, to inspire virtuous impulses, and to impart strength to endure trial and resist temptation. (Grace | Definition, Description, Christianity, & Beliefs, n.d.)

There are several types of grace, each with its own unique characteristics and implications. Common grace refers to the blessings that God bestows upon all of humanity, regardless of their faith or works of righteousness. (Common grace - Wikipedia, n.d.) This includes the beauty of nature, the joy of relationships, and the sustenance provided by the earth. It is the grace that allows the sun to rise on both the just and the unjust, a testament to the impartial benevolence of the divine. (What does Matthew 5:45 mean?, n.d.) Saving grace, on the other hand, is a more specific, personal and profound manifestation. (O'Callaghan et al., 2024) It is the grace that redeems and reconciles, offering salvation and eternal life to those who accept it. This Grace is the reason for Jesus coming into the world and his doctrines, teaching and emphasizing the belief that salvation is a gift from God, not a reward for human effort. (Matthew 19:25 When the disciples heard this, they were greatly astonished and asked, "Who then can be saved?", n.d.) It is through saving grace that individuals are believed to be justified and sanctified, transformed from a state of sin to one of righteousness in Christ Jesus. (Justification and Sanctification, n.d.)

Another form of grace is Sanctifying grace, which is said to dwell within the soul, enabling individuals to grow in holiness and virtue. (Sanctifying Grace, n.d.) It is the grace that empowers believers to live according to God divine will, fostering a deeper relationship with Jesus and all of humanity. Sanctifying grace is often viewed as a continuous process, a journey of spiritual growth and moral development. The concept of actual grace refers to the temporary divine interventions that assist individuals in specific situations. (Actual Grace - PopeHistory.com, n.d.) These are the moments of clarity, strength, or inspiration that guide individuals through challenges and temptations. Then there is Actual grace, which is seen as the divine nudge that helps individuals make choices aligned with their higher purpose. To illustrate the impact of grace, consider the story of a person who, despite a life filled with hardship and poor choices, experiences a profound transformation. This individual, once lost in a cycle of despair and self-destruction, encounters a moment of grace (clarity) that alters their trajectory. It might be a chance encounter with a compassionate stranger, an unexpected opportunity for redemption, or a sudden realization of their inherent worth.

The joy of grace is another aspect that warrants exploration. Grace brings with it a sense of peace and contentment, a release from the burdens of guilt and the relentless pursuit of perfection. It allows individuals to accept their imperfections and to find beauty in their humanity. The joy of grace is the realization that one is loved and valued, not for what they have done, but for who they are. It is the freedom to live authentically, to embrace one's true self without fear of judgment or rejection. In a world often characterized by competition and comparison, grace offers a different paradigm. It invites individuals to step off the treadmill of achievement and to rest in the assurance of unconditional love. This does not mean that effort and ambition are without value, but rather that they are not the ultimate determinants of one's worth. Grace reminds us that we are enough, just as we are, and that our value is inherent and immutable. The implications of grace extend beyond the individual, influencing communities and societies as a whole. A culture of grace fosters an environment of acceptance and compassion, where individuals are encouraged to support and uplift one another. It challenges systems of inequality and injustice, advocating for a world where everyone is treated with dignity and respect.

Grace calls for a radical reimagining of relationships, where forgiveness and understanding replace judgment and condemnation. Consider the case study of a community that embraces the principles of grace. In this community, individuals are encouraged to share their struggles and vulnerabilities without fear of shame or ostracism. The focus is on mutual support and growth, with members actively seeking ways to help one another thrive. Conflicts are addressed with empathy and a willingness to forgive, recognizing that everyone is on a journey of learning and development. This community becomes a beacon of hope and healing, demonstrating the transformative power of grace in action. From a broader perspective, grace can be seen as a divine invitation to participate in a higher reality, one that transcends the limitations of the material world. It is an invitation to experience the fullness of life, to connect with the divine, and to become co-creators of a more just and loving world. Grace calls individuals to rise above their circumstances, to see beyond the immediate challenges, and to embrace a vision of what could be.

In conclusion, the nature of grace is a profound and multifaceted concept that defies simple explanation. It is a gift that transforms, heals, and empowers, offering a glimpse of the divine love that underpins all of creation. Whether experienced as common grace, saving grace, sanctifying grace, or actual grace, it is a force that invites individuals to live with purpose, joy, and compassion. As we continue to explore the saving grace of God in this book, let us remain open to the possibilities that grace presents, and to the transformative power it holds for each of us and for the world.

## The Nature of Grace

The Merriam-Webster Dictionary defines *grace* as "unmerited divine assistance given to humans for their regeneration or sanctification; a virtue coming from God; a state of sanctification enjoyed through divine assistance." (Grace, 2025) By definition, "unmerited" means "not earned, not deserved, and not owed." (unmerited, n.d.) Thus, grace is the free and undeserved favor of God, given at His expense for the eternal benefit of the recipient. It is priceless, beyond all measure, and cannot be purchased by human effort or merit.

Scripture reveals many expressions of God's grace, mercy, pardon, favor, kindness, compassion, clemency, charity, and more. (Topical Bible: Graciousness and Compassion, n.d.) Yet the grace of God is not limited to these expressions; it is infinite and experienced by all in one form or another.

From the beginning, when Adam transgressed in the Garden of Eden, humanity's fellowship with God was severed. (Sermon: Genesis 3:22-24: Adam Driven Out, n.d.) In that act of disobedience, humanity became spiritually dead, separated from its Source of life. (Ephesians 2:1-22, n.d.) Adam and Eve became "dead in spirit," alive in body but cut off from the life of God. (Death, n.d.) Death, in its truest sense, is separation from God; without the spirit, there is no life. (Death | Bible.org, n.d.)

Adam was God's son by creation; Christ however is God's Son by birth, eternal generation, the only begotten of the Father. The Son of God, who created all things, entered His creation to redeem fallen humanity. He bore the penalty of our sin and restored what Adam had lost. The price He paid is beyond human comprehension, priceless, infinite, and eternal in its value.

## An Illustration of Saving Grace

The New Testament gives a vivid picture of this grace in the account of Saul of Tarsus. Once a fierce persecutor of the Church, Saul consented to the stoning of Stephen and sought to imprison and kill followers of Christ. Yet on the road to Damascus, Saul encountered the risen Lord Jesus, who called him by name and transformed him from an enemy of the Gospel into its chief ambassador to the Gentiles. (Acts 9:1-19, n.d.) This radical transformation is nothing less than the saving grace of God in action (Acts 6–9).

In truth, every day we awaken to life is an act of divine grace. Whether righteous or unrighteous, believer or unbeliever, each breath we take is a testament to God's mercy and grace. His existence does not depend on our acknowledgment or belief; He is the Almighty, the self-existent One, whose grace is poured out upon all humanity.

We are recipients of this grace solely because of the work of Christ on the cross. We could never earn it; the debt was beyond our ability to pay. Yet God, in His love, has freely given it through His Son. This is the beauty and the glory of grace; it is the gift of God to all mankind.

## A Testimony of God's Preserving Grace

Permit me to recount, to the best of my recollection, a true account from my early life; one that I believe serves as a vivid testimony of the grace of God. I am a twin, and while I am deeply thankful for all my siblings, my sister and I share a bond marked by many parallel experiences. What I now share spans from our birth to our early childhood, and I trust it will help illustrate the nature of divine grace.

Family members have told me that my sister and I were born within a short span of one another, perhaps six minutes, fifteen, or even thirty. Exact details vary among those who once recounted the story, and many have since gone to their eternal rest. Shortly after my birth, I was taken home, but within approximately two weeks I was rushed back to the hospital, gravely ill with pneumonia. I was placed in an incubator for what some said was two months, while others maintained it was closer to six.

During this time, my mother and grandmother told me that I ceased breathing on two occasions and that the attending physician successfully resuscitated me each time. Though the precise details are now veiled by time, I know that my life hung in the balance more than once in those early days.

My sister, too, faced a perilous brush with death at a very young age. When she was about one or two years old, she accidentally swallowed a small clock wheel from a wristwatch, a metal piece with ridged edges essential for the turning of the watch's hands. She began to choke, turning blue, when the doctor struck her back and expelled the obstruction, sparing her life.

Thus, in the earliest chapters of our lives, both my sister and I came face to face with the shadow of death, yet by the providence of God, our lives were preserved. Scripture teaches that "the wages of sin is death" (Romans

6:23), and because of the fall of Adam and Eve in Eden, death holds rightful claim over all humanity. Yet the same verse declares that "the gift of God is eternal life through Jesus Christ our Lord." This unearned and undeserved favor, grace, was manifested to us, not only in the offer of eternal salvation but in the granting of continued earthly life.

I must also note the instrument God chose for our deliverance. The attending physician was a white man, something notable in that era when such compassionate care for Black children was far from common. My mother recalled that he was determined that I should live, and his skill and persistence were the means by which God spared me. I believe the same doctor intervened in my sister's case as well.

To God alone belongs the glory for using this man as an instrument of His mercy. Our survival was not due to any merit of our own but was a demonstration of God's sovereign will that we should live to fulfill the purpose He ordained for us before the foundation of the world. Truly, our lives are living testimonies to the grace of God, grace that preserves, sustains, and appoints us for His glory.

These events remind me that, because of Adam's sin, we all deserve death; yet by God's unmerited favor, we live. Life itself is a gracious gift, granted for the fulfillment of God's purposes. The Lord has preserved my sister and me for His glory, and to Him alone belongs the praise.

Grace is an intangible gift of profound significance, power, and worth, utterly essential for every human life. Deprived of grace, we are left without true hope or purpose; our very reason for living is diminished. Yet, grace has been generously bestowed upon all people, and we encounter its influence each day. Therefore, let us give thanks to God through Jesus Christ our Lord for the wondrous gift of grace. One of the most remarkable aspects of grace is that it is not only received but can also be freely given and shared with others. The giving of grace does not require justification; it asks only for humility and love. With these qualities, we are able to extend the extraordinary blessing of grace to everyone we meet.

The value, purpose, power, and love inherent in grace transcend the limits of human imagination. Yet God, in His mercy, has created a new creature, a new creation, to house the spirit and soul of every person who confesses Jesus Christ as Lord with their mouth and believes in their heart that God raised Him from the dead. Such individuals will be saved from God's wrath and will inherit this newly created body, enabling them to enjoy the full value, purpose, power, and love of God's Grace for all eternity. Now, let us look at some of the inherent value, purpose, power, and love in grace.

## Grace as Undeserved Kindness

At its core, grace is often defined as undeserved kindness. This aspect of grace is perhaps the most foundational, serving as the bedrock upon which other dimensions of grace are built. The concept of undeserved kindness challenges the human tendency to equate worthiness with merit. In many religious traditions, grace is seen as a gift bestowed by the divine, not because of any inherent goodness or achievement on the part of the recipient, but purely out of benevolence and love. (The Father of the Prodigal Son, n.d.) Consider the parable of the prodigal son, a narrative that exemplifies undeserved kindness. (Yes, The Parable of the Prodigal Son Is Unfair and Uncomfortable, n.d.) In this story, a wayward son squanders his inheritance on reckless living, only to return home destitute and repentant. Rather than meting out punishment or demanding restitution, the father welcomes him with open arms, celebrating his return with a feast.

This act of grace defies human logic, emphasizing that divine kindness transcends human notions of justice and retribution. (Meditation on Divine Mercy and Justice - Part 3, n.d.) The implications of grace as undeserved kindness are profound. It suggests that no one is beyond the reach of divine love and that redemption is available to all, regardless of past transgressions. (Bible Study: Luke 15 The Prodigal Son- A Journey of Grace and Redemption, n.d.) This perspective fosters a sense of humility and gratitude, encouraging individuals to extend kindness and forgiveness to others, mirroring the divine example. In a world often marked by judgment and exclusion, the principle of undeserved kindness offers a radical alternative, inviting individuals to embrace a more compassionate and inclusive worldview.

**Grace in Forgiveness**
Forgiveness is another critical dimension of saving grace, offering a pathway to healing and reconciliation. The act of forgiving, whether receiving or extending it, is a profound expression of grace that has the power to transform relationships and restore brokenness. In many religious traditions, forgiveness is seen as a divine mandate, reflecting the grace that individuals have received from Christ. (Christian Forgiveness: A Biblical Mandate Rooted in Divine Example, n.d.) The story of the woman

caught in adultery provides a compelling example of grace in forgiveness. (Who Was The Woman Caught In Adultery In The Bible?, n.d.) When brought before Jesus, the accusers demanded punishment according to the law. However, Jesus responded with compassion, challenging those without sin to cast the first stone. His words prompted the accusers to leave, and he offered the woman forgiveness, encouraging her to live a transformed life. (Lesson 45: Caught in the Act (John 7:53-8:11), n.d.)

This narrative highlights the liberating power of grace, which breaks the cycle of condemnation and offers a new beginning. Forgiveness, as an expression of grace, is not limited to interpersonal relationships but extends to self-forgiveness as well. (Baum & Cindy, n.d.) Many individuals struggle with feelings of guilt and shame, burdened by past mistakes and failures. (Guilt and Shame, n.d.) Embracing grace in forgiveness allows individuals to release these burdens, accepting the divine invitation to start anew. This process is not always easy, requiring courage and vulnerability, but it is essential for personal growth and spiritual renewal. Furthermore, grace in forgiveness challenges societal norms that prioritize retribution and punishment. It calls for a paradigm shift, advocating for restorative justice and reconciliation. (Breaking Out: The Expansiveness of Restorative Justice in Laudato Si', n.d.) By prioritizing healing over vengeance, grace in forgiveness fosters a more compassionate and just society, reflecting the divine intention for humanity.

## Grace as Patience

Grace as patience is an essential aspect of divine interaction with humanity, reflecting the enduring forbearance and long-suffering nature of God. This dimension of grace acknowledges human fallibility and the propensity for error, yet it offers a compassionate response that transcends immediate judgment or retribution. In many religious traditions, divine patience is seen as an expression of love, allowing individuals the time and space to grow, learn, and ultimately transform. (Topical Bible: Divine Patience and Judgment, n.d.) Consider the biblical narrative of the Israelites' journey through the wilderness, a story that exemplifies grace as patience. (Acts 13:18 He endured their conduct for about forty years in the wilderness., n.d.) Despite repeated instances of disobedience and doubt, God's divine presence remained steadfast, guiding them towards the Promised Land. (Acts 13:18 He endured their conduct for about forty years in the wilderness., n.d.)

This enduring patience underscores the belief that divine grace is not contingent upon human perfection but is instead a constant, unwavering force that accompanies individuals on their spiritual journey. In practical terms, grace as patience manifests itself in the lives of every individual who is given the opportunity to learn from their mistakes and to pursue personal growth without the fear of immediate condemnation. This aspect of grace encourages a spirit of perseverance and resilience, fostering an environment where individuals can strive for improvement and transformation. Moreover, it challenges societal norms that prioritize immediate results and perfection, advocating instead for a more compassionate and understanding approach to personal development.

Furthermore, grace as patience invites individuals to extend the same forbearance to others, mirroring the divine example. By cultivating a spirit of patience, individuals can foster healthier relationships and create a more harmonious community, reflecting the divine intention for humanity. This perspective encourages a shift from judgment to understanding, promoting a culture of empathy and support.

## Grace as Provision

Another critical dimension of divine grace is its role as provision, offering sustenance and support in times of need. This aspect of grace acknowledges the inherent limitations of human resources and the necessity of divine intervention to meet the needs of individuals and communities. In many religious traditions, grace as provision is seen as a testament to the divine's generosity and care for creation. (Grace | Definition, Description, Christianity, & Beliefs, n.d.) The story of Elijah and the widow of Zarephath provide a compelling example of grace as provision. (Elijah and the Widow: A Lesson in Divine Provision, n.d.) During a time of severe famine, Elijah encountered a widow who was preparing to make her last meal with the little flour and oil she had left. Through divine intervention, her resources were miraculously multiplied, sustaining her household throughout the famine. (30 Great Examples of Divine Intervention In The Bible, n.d.)

This narrative highlights the belief that divine grace is a source of abundance, capable of meeting the needs of those who trust in its provision. In contemporary contexts, grace as provision can be seen in various forms, such as unexpected financial assistance, opportunities for employment, or the support of a caring community. (Emergency Assistance – GRACE Grapevine, n.d.) These instances of divine provision serve as reminders of the constant presence and care of our Lord, reinforcing the belief that individuals are never alone in their struggles. Moreover, grace as provision encourages a posture of gratitude and generosity, inviting individuals to share their resources with others and to participate in God's work of caring for creation.

This dimension of grace also challenges societal narratives that equate worth with material wealth, proposing instead a perspective that values contentment and gratitude. By recognizing the sufficiency of divine provision, individuals can cultivate a spirit of trust and reliance on God, fostering a deeper sense of connection and purpose to him.

## Grace as Protection

Grace as protection is another vital aspect of divine grace, offering a sense of safety and security in the midst of life's uncertainties. This dimension of grace acknowledges the inherent risks and dangers of a person, both physical and spiritual experience, yet it provides a shield against harm, reflecting the divine's commitment to safeguarding creation. In many religious traditions, grace as protection is seen as an expression of divine love and care, offering reassurance and peace to those who trust in God's Power. (Divine grace, n.d.) The story of Daniel in the lion's den serves as a powerful illustration of grace as protection. (Daniel In The Lion's Den: Miracle Of Protection, n.d.) Despite being thrown into a den of lions for his unwavering faith, Daniel emerged unharmed, protected by divine intervention. (Daniel in the lions' den, n.d.)

This narrative underscores the belief that divine

grace is a source of refuge and strength, capable of delivering individuals from perilous situations. In practical terms, grace as protection can be experienced in various ways, such as the prevention of accidents, the healing of illnesses, or the guidance away from dangerous paths. (120 Divine Prayers for Protection and Safety, n.d.) These instances of divine protection serve as reminders of the constant vigilance and care of God, reinforcing the belief that individuals are never abandoned in their times of need. Moreover, grace as protection encourages a spirit of courage and confidence, empowering individuals to face challenges with the assurance of divine support. This aspect of grace also challenges societal narratives that prioritize self-reliance and control, advocating instead for a perspective that values trust and surrender. By recognizing the protective power of divine grace, individuals can cultivate a spirit of peace and security, fostering a deeper sense of connection and trust in the Lord.

**Grace as Deliverance**

Another role to be explored is grace as deliverance, offering liberation from the burdens and constraints of life. This aspect of grace acknowledges the inherent struggles and challenges of the human condition, providing a pathway to freedom and renewal. In many religious traditions, grace as deliverance is seen as a testament to the divine's power to overcome obstacles and transform lives. (The Divine Transforming Grace, n.d.) The story of the Exodus, where the Israelites were delivered from slavery in Egypt, serves as a powerful illustration of grace as deliverance. (Walt & D., 2026) Despite the overwhelming odds and the might of Pharaoh's army, the divine intervention led to their liberation and journey towards the Promised Land.

This narrative underscores the belief that divine grace has the power to break chains and set individuals free from the constraints that bind them. In contemporary contexts, grace as deliverance can be experienced in various forms, such as the release from addiction, the healing of emotional wounds, or the breaking of cycles of poverty and oppression. These instances of divine deliverance serve as reminders of the constant presence and power of Almighty God, reinforcing the belief that individuals are never without hope in their struggles.

Moreover, grace as deliverance encourages a spirit of resilience and perseverance, inviting individuals to trust in the transformative power of God. This dimension of grace challenges societal narratives that prioritize self-reliance and control, advocating instead for a perspective that values surrender and trust. By recognizing the deliverance of divine grace, individuals can cultivate a spirit of freedom and renewal, fostering a deeper sense of connection and liberation in their lives. The transformative dimensions of grace as inner peace, guidance, empowerment for good works, and deliverance offer a comprehensive understanding of its profound impact on the human experience.

These aspects of grace provide a framework for individuals to navigate the complexities of life with hope and resilience, offering the promise of divine support and empowerment. As a divine invitation, grace extends to all, offering the opportunity to embrace a life marked by compassion, gratitude, and trust in the Lord. It is a gift that transcends human understanding, inviting individuals to participate in the divine work of transforming the world.

## Grace as Hope for the Future

Another critical dimension of divine grace is its role as a source of hope for the future. This aspect of grace acknowledges the inherent uncertainties and challenges of life, offering a vision of possibility and promise that transcends present circumstances. In many religious traditions, grace as hope for the future is seen as a testament to God's unwavering commitment to the well-being and flourishing of creation. (Divine grace, n.d.) The story of the prophet Jeremiah provides a compelling example of grace as hope for the future. Amidst the destruction and despair of the Babylonian exile, Jeremiah delivered a message of hope, proclaiming that the Lord had plans for his people's welfare and not for harm, to give them a future with hope. (The Real Biblical Meaning of Jeremiah 29:11, n.d.)

This narrative underscores the belief that divine grace offers a vision of a better tomorrow, providing the strength and courage needed to persevere through difficult times. In contemporary contexts, grace as hope for the future can be experienced in various forms, such as the resilience to overcome adversity, the inspiration to pursue dreams, or the assurance of a brighter future. These instances of hope serve as reminders of the constant presence and care of God, reinforcing the belief that individuals are never without hope in their struggles. Moreover, grace as hope for the future encourages a spirit of optimism and perseverance, inviting individuals to trust in the unfolding of God's divine plan for humanity.

This dimension of grace challenges societal narratives that equate hope with certainty and control, advocating instead for a perspective that values trust and surrender. By recognizing the hope that divine grace offers, individuals can cultivate a spirit of faith and resilience, fostering a deeper sense of connection and trust in the Almighty God.

## Grace as Unmerited Favor

Grace as unmerited favor is a foundational aspect of divine grace, reflecting the belief that grace is a gift freely given, not based on merit or worthiness. (The Concept of Grace: Understanding God's Unmerited Favor, n.d.) This dimension of grace acknowledges the inherent limitations and imperfections of the human condition, offering acceptance and love without conditions. In many religious traditions, grace as unmerited favor is seen as a testament to the Lord boundless generosity and compassion. The parable of the laborers in the vineyard provides a powerful illustration of grace as unmerited favor. In this story, laborers are hired at different times throughout the day, yet all receive the same wage. This act of generosity defies human notions of fairness and justice, emphasizing that divine grace is not earned but freely given. (The Laborers in the Vineyard, n.d.) Consider, too, the story of Jesus Christ, His fulfillment of the Father's will and His redemptive work. Through His sacrifice on the cross, He accomplished the purpose for which He came: to pay the price for the redemption of all humanity. (Cross and Resurrection in Work, n.d.)

This narrative highlights the belief that divine grace extends to all, regardless of their past actions or achievements. In practical terms, grace as unmerited favor can manifest in various ways, such as the experience of unconditional love, the acceptance of one's imperfections, or the opportunity for a fresh start. These instances of favor serve as reminders of the constant presence and love of God, reinforcing the belief that individuals are never beyond the reach of grace. Moreover, grace as unmerited favor encourages a spirit of humility and gratitude, inviting individuals to extend the same acceptance and love to others.

This dimension of grace challenges societal narratives that equate worth with achievement and status, proposing instead a perspective that values acceptance and compassion. By recognizing the unmerited favor of God's grace, individuals can cultivate a spirit of generosity and inclusivity, fostering a deeper sense of connection and belonging for God.

**Grace as Eternal Life**

The final dimension of divine grace to be explored is its role as the promise of eternal life. This aspect of grace acknowledges the inherent transience and mortality of the human condition, offering the assurance of a life beyond the physical realm. In the Christian Faith, grace as eternal life is seen as a testament to God's desire for eternal communion with all of humanity; his creation. The story of the resurrection of Jesus serves as a powerful illustration of grace as eternal life. Despite the finality of death, the resurrection offers the promise of new life and the assurance of eternal communion with God for every believer. (Eternal Life | Cru, n.d.)

This narrative underscores the belief that divine grace, the saving grace of God, transcends the limitations of the physical world, offering the hope of eternal life in His present. This hope of eternal life serves as a reminder of the Lord God constant presence and his promises which reinforces the belief that individuals are never without hope in the face of mortality.

Moreover, grace as eternal life encourages a spirit of faith and trust, inviting individuals to embrace the mystery of God. This dimension of grace challenges societal narratives that equate life with the physical and temporal, advocating instead for a perspective that values the spiritual and eternal. By recognizing the promise of eternal life through divine grace, individuals can cultivate a spirit of hope and transcendence, fostering a deeper sense of connection and purpose. In conclusion, the transformative dimensions of grace as transformation, hope for the future, unmerited favor, and eternal life offer a comprehensive understanding of its profound impact on the human race and their experiences.

These aspects of grace provide a framework for individuals to navigate the complexities of life with hope and resilience, offering the promise of divine support and empowerment. As a divine invitation, grace extends to all, offering the opportunity to embrace a life marked by compassion, gratitude, love and trust in the Lord our God. It is a gift that transcends human understanding, inviting individuals to participate in God's divine work of transforming the world.

‹ CHAPTER 2 ›

# GRACE THROUGH JESUS CHRIST

*In* order to apprehend the means by which we receive grace through Jesus Christ, it is incumbent upon us first to contemplate His identity and the manner of His incarnation. The Gospel according to John opens with a profound declaration concerning His eternal nature:

> *"In the beginning [before all time] was the Word (Christ), and the Word was with God, and the Word was God Himself. He was [continually existing] in the beginning [co-eternally] with God. All things were made and came into existence through Him; and without Him not even one thing was made that has come into being. In Him was life [and the power to bestow life], and the life was the Light of men. The Light shines on in the darkness, and the darkness did not understand it or overpower it or appropriate it or absorb it [and is unreceptive to it]." (John 1:1–5, AMP)*

These sacred verses proclaim that before the foundation of the world, indeed, before time itself, there existed the Lord God, His Word, and His Spirit. The Word, who is Jesus the Christ, was not a created being, but was eternally with God and, in very essence, was God. It is through this divine Word that all things came into being; nothing exists apart from His creative will and power. Thus, Jesus Christ co-existed eternally with the Father and the Holy Spirit, one in essence, yet distinct in Person. In Him resides the fullness of life, and He Himself is the Light of the world. This Light dispels the darkness, for the darkness neither comprehends, overcomes, nor subdues it. The radiance of Christ's Light remains unconquered, eternally triumphant over all that is opposed to God.

## The Fall of Humanity and God's Redemptive Plan

Let us return to that momentous occasion in the Garden of Eden, the fall of humanity. From the very moment of man's transgression, the Almighty set in motion His eternal plan to redeem those whom He had created in His image and after His likeness; those to whom He had entrusted dominion over the works of His hands, this physical world. A world which God Himself had created and pronounced "good" was plunged into corruption and disorder by the disobedience of Adam and Eve, bringing forth chaos, destruction, and every manner of evil. Yet such was the greatness of God's love for humanity that He ordained a plan of redemption to reconcile mankind unto Himself. This redemptive purpose was first declared in the Garden of Eden, when God spoke of the Seed of the woman who would bruise the serpent's head (Genesis 3:15). The righteousness with which man had been endowed at creation became defiled through sin, thereby necessitating a costly atonement. Though man had been made upright, Scripture declares,

> *"all our righteousnesses are as filthy rags"*
> *(Isaiah 64:6).*

Adam, the son of God by creation, through his act of disobedience corrupted not only his own nature but also that of all his descendants. By eating of the tree of the knowledge of good and evil, humanity inherited both the awareness and the propensity for evil, resulting in a separation from God, our Creator. Thus, in Adam's fall all humanity became unrighteous, for all were in his loins. As it is written in Isaiah 64:4–6 (NKJV):

> *"For since the beginning of the world Men have not heard nor perceived by the ear, Nor has the eye seen any God besides You, Who acts for the one who waits for Him. You meet him who rejoices and does righteousness, Who remembers You in Your ways. You are indeed angry, for we have sinned In these ways we continue; And we need to be saved. But we are all like an unclean thing, And all our righteousnesses are like filthy rags; We all fade as a leaf, And our iniquities, like the wind, Have taken us away."*

This passage reveals the true condition of mankind: by nature we are unclean and unrighteous, having forfeited the fullness of the divine image and likeness. We have lost our way. Yet thanks be to God, who in His mercy has provided redemption for all who will receive it. For the Word of God declares in Romans 10:13 (NKJV),

> *"For whoever calls on the name of the Lord shall be saved."*

This gracious promise extends to every person, regardless of race, color, gender, or nationality.

Since the fall of man in the Garden of Eden, and from the days of the flood until the coming of the Lord,

God has spoken to humanity through His chosen servants: Kings, Priests, Judges, and Prophets of old, concerning the promise of a coming Savior. This person who is the Messiah, the Christ, will give His life as a ransom for many to redeem mankind back to God. From the beginning, the divine plan of God was that His Son would come forth, not as a created being, but born of a virgin woman who had never known or lay with a man. In this manner, the Father would reveal the way of salvation and proclaim the Kingdom of Heaven, so that all might be saved through Him, should they choose to believe.

The Gospel according to Saint John opens with the solemn declaration:

*"In the beginning was the Word, and the Word was with God, and the Word was God."*

Before all creation, the Word existed eternally with God and was God. This Word, the eternal Logos, was made flesh, taking upon Himself human nature, and entered the world as the Christ, the Son of God. The Son was begotten, not made, for He Himself is the Creator of all things; thus, He cannot be a created being. In the creation account, God made Adam, and within him, all humanity was represented. Even Eve, the mother of all Human Beings, was formed from Adam's rib when God caused him to fall into a deep sleep and took one of his ribs from him and closed up the flesh where He took the rib, and fashioned the woman from Adam rib. Not only was the physical body of the female Adam taken from the male Adam but the essence that is the spirit and soul of the female Adam was taken from the male Adam as well. We know this to be true because of what Adam said in Genesis Chapter 2, and verse 23.

*"And Adam said, This is now bone of my bones, and flesh of my flesh: she shall be called Woman, **because she was taken out of Man**."*

God extracted the spirit and soul of Eve, the female Adam from the male Adam that He breathed the breath of life in through his nostrils. Every part of us, spirit, soul, and body, came forth from our ancestors through our parents. So, what is it to God to take from the male (Adam) what he breathes or put into him, the female (Adam/Eve)? For Adam, God directly created and gave life. For his descendants, life (body, soul, spirit) is transmitted through parents, but God is still seen as the ultimate source and sustainer of life. So, for God to give or take breath (life) is not difficult, it is the natural exercise of His creative and sustaining power, whether directly (as with Adam) or indirectly (as with us through our ancestry).

Nevertheless, we can see in this verse that all mankind was in Adam from the beginning of creation. Yet though we were created in Adam, we come into being or the world, by birth. For this reason, it was necessary that Christ also be born; coming into the world as man, fully sharing our humanity, while remaining fully God as the eternal Son of the Father. Scripture affirms this in Luke 1:30-32 that says,

*"Then the angel said to her, "Do not be afraid, Mary, for you have found favor with God. And behold, you will conceive in your womb and bring forth a Son, and shall call His name Jesus. He will be great, and will be*

*called the Son of the Highest; and the Lord
God will give Him the throne of His father
David." (NKJV)*

Thus, the incarnate Word, Jesus Christ, took on human
flesh to accomplish the will of the Father and fulfill His
redemptive purpose for mankind.

The mystery of His incarnation was revealed when
the angel Gabriel appeared to the Virgin Mary, declaring
that she would conceive and bear a Son, and that His name
would be called *Emmanuel*, meaning *God with us*. Mary,
being betrothed to Joseph but having known no man,
questioned how such a thing could be. The angel Gabriel
announced that the Holy Spirit would come upon her, and
the power of the Most High would overshadow her, so that
the holy One to be born would be called the Son of God.
Mary received this word in faith, and in due time, by the
miraculous work of God, she conceived in her womb the
Lord Jesus Christ. After the appointed time was fulfilled,
she brought forth her first born child, the Son of God and
named Him Jesus, the Christ, the promised Redeemer.

Sacred Scripture presents a rich tapestry of prophetic
revelation concerning the advent of the Messiah. The
biblical record not only foretells His birth, ministry,
suffering, death by crucifixion, burial, and resurrection, but
also traces His divine lineage, rooted in Abraham,
established through David, and realized in His earthly
parents, Joseph and Mary. From the very beginning, in the
Garden of Eden, the promise of redemption was declared;
thus, the coming of Jesus Christ was not accidental, but the
eternal and sovereign design of Almighty God to send a
Savior for the redemption of all who believe in Him, even

his Name.

### *The prophet Micah, under divine inspiration, declared:*

*"But you, Bethlehem Ephrathah, Though you are little among the thousands of Judah, Yet out of you shall come forth to Me The One to be Ruler in Israel, Whose goings forth are from of old, From everlasting." (Micah 5:2, NKJV).*

The covenant promises were further reinforced through the Davidic line. Although King David was of the tribe of Judah, the prophetic word spoke of a righteous Branch arising from his house. Jeremiah proclaimed:

*" 'Behold, the days are coming,' says the Lord, That I will raise to David a Branch of righteousness; A King shall reign and prosper, And execute judgment and righteousness in the earth." (Jeremiah 23:5, NKJV).*

The Easy-to-Read Version read this way,

### *The Good "Branch"*

*"This message is from the Lord: The time is coming, when I will raise up a good 'branch' from David's family. He will be a king who will rule in a wise way. He will do what is fair and right in the land."*

The typology of Christ is also foreshadowed in the patriarch Abraham. When tested by God upon Mount

Moriah, Abraham's willingness to offer up his beloved son Isaac prefigured the ultimate sacrifice of Christ, the Son of God. In response to Abraham's faith and obedience, the Lord declared that all nations of the earth would be blessed through his seed, the ultimate fulfillment of this promise founded in the person of God's Son, is fulfilled in Jesus Christ (Genesis 22:9–18).

Moreover, the prophecy of Balaam in the book of Numbers anticipates the coming Messiah:

> "I see Him, but not now; I behold Him, but not near; A Star shall come out of Jacob; A Scepter shall rise out of Israel, And batter the brow of Moab, And destroy all the sons of tumult....Out of Jacob One shall have dominion, And destroy the remains of the city." (Numbers 24:17, 19, NKJV).

Taken together, these prophecies reveal that the mission of Jesus Christ was foreordained from eternity. His coming was the fulfillment of divine promise, the outworking of God's redemptive plan, and the ultimate demonstration of covenant faithfulness.

**Jesus as I Am**

How does Grace tie into Jesus Christ and him being the savior? To help us understand how Grace comes through Jesus Christ, let us examine the nature of Jesus to see who He truly is. Let us explore Jesus as the "I Am." I recall reading a story about Moses, born to Levite parents and hidden by his mother for three months. After she could no longer hide him, she placed him in a basket and sent him down the river, where Pharaoh's daughter found him, had compassion on him, and arranged for his own mother to nurse him. He was raised as Pharaoh's daughter's son and she named him Moses because she drew him from the water. As an adult, Moses witnessed the mistreatment of his people, killed an Egyptian in their defense, and fled to Midian when Pharaoh sought his life. In Midian, Moses married Zipporah, daughter of Jethro, a priest. When the Israelites cried out to God under Egyptian bondage, God remembered His covenant with their ancestors. Moses, meanwhile, was tending Jethro's flock near the mountain of God in Horeb.

At Horeb, an angel appeared to Moses in a burning bush that was not consumed. God spoke, revealing His intent to send Moses to Egypt to free Israel, despite Moses' reluctance. When Moses inquired about God's name, God replied, 'I AM THAT I AM,' reinforcing God's eternal presence, a foundational truth that underpins grace, later embodied by Jesus. The words "I Am" in Hebrew is **"Ehyeh (אֶהְיֶה)**: This is the first-person singular future perfect tense of the verb "to be," meaning "I will be" or "I exist." (Discovering Your Real Name, n.d.) With this name, God reveals a fundamental aspect of His eternal nature. (Arnold & Mark, 2019) One of the meanings of the word 'Am' is 'Exist,' reminding us that God's presence and existence are vital to all believers and assisting in understanding His grace through Jesus Christ. (What is the meaning of God's name, "I AM WHO I AM"?, n.d.)

## Jesus as Deliverer

Although there is no scripture that explicitly states Jesus as a deliverer, there are scriptures that convey the concept and his work of delivering the people of God. Let us explore a few scriptures to explain this concept. Take

Isaiah 61:1, which talks about Jesus' purpose for coming: "to preach the gospel to the meek; to bind up the brokenhearted, proclaim liberty to the captives, and the opening of the prison to those that are bound." God anointed Jesus to do a great work for his kingdom and the people of God.

Then there is Isaiah 12:2-3, which speaks of God as our "salvation, and the Lord Jehovah as our strength, our song and the water of our salvation." In 1 Thessalonians Chapter 1, Verse 10, speaks of Jesus as "the one who delivered us from the wrath of God that is to come." And in Colossians 1:13-14, it speaks of God through Jesus Christ, which reads,

> *"He has delivered us from the power of darkness and conveyed us into the kingdom of the Son of His love, in whom we have redemption through His blood, the forgiveness of sins." New King James Version.*

Yes, Jesus is truly our deliverer from the snare of the fowler, the pestilence, and the deceitfulness of our enemy, whose purpose is to steal, kill, and destroy God's people and creation; this enemy is Satan and his demons.

### Jesus as "Redeemer"

When one reflects upon the designation of Jesus Christ as Redeemer, it becomes evident that this title holds profound significance for understanding the divine plan of salvation and for the spiritual life of all believers. A comprehensive grasp of the concept of redemption is therefore essential, for it illuminates both the nature of God's saving work and our response as recipients of His grace. At this stage of spiritual formation, knowledge of Jesus Christ and the apprehension of grace through Him form's the foundational elements of Christian growth and maturity in relationship to God the Father and His Son, Jesus Christ.

To proceed, it is prudent to clarify the terms under consideration. The verb "to redeem" denotes the act of buying back or repurchasing; it implies the recovery or reclamation of something that was lost or alienated. Correspondingly, a "redeemer" is one who performs this act, effecting restoration through the payment of a price. With these definitions in place, we may now establish the theological groundwork for understanding how grace is mediated through Jesus Christ. Sacred Scripture affirms that Jesus is the Word of God, the Creator of all things, and that nothing exists apart from Him (cf. John 1:1-3). As the Creator, Christ possesses inherent ownership and sovereignty over all creation.

Yet, the narrative in Genesis recounts that God created humanity in His own image and likeness, bestowing upon Adam dominion over the works of His hands. Adam, as God's son by creation, was granted authority over the earth, thereby occupying a unique position as the steward, indeed, the god (with a lowercase 'g'), of this world. God established a garden as Adam's dwelling and entrusted him with the responsibility to cultivate and guard it. Within the garden, two trees held particular significance: the Tree of Life and the Tree of the Knowledge of Good and Evil. God commanded Adam that he could freely eat from every tree except the tree of the knowledge of good and evil, warning that transgression would result in death. Adam's wife, created as his companion and helper, was ultimately deceived by the serpent, leading both her and Adam to disobey God's command.

Through this act of disobedience, they experienced spiritual death, fell from divine favor, and became estranged from their source of life. This original transgression led to the fall of humanity, prompting God to initiate His redemptive plan to restore humankind to Himself. To accomplish this, God sent His Word, his only begotten Son, Jesus Christ, to pay the price necessary for humanity's redemption.

The motif of the Redeemer is evident even in the Old Testament. Job declares, "I know that my Redeemer lives" (Job 19:25), affirming his faith in a living Redeemer, a passage often interpreted in Christian theology as pointing to Christ Himself. The apostle Paul writes of Jesus in Ephesians 1:7,

> *"In whom we have redemption through his blood, the forgiveness of sins, according to the riches of his grace;"*

Thus, Christ's sacrificial death is seen as the means by which believers are reconciled to God and granted the forgiveness of sins. Through His crucifixion, burial, and resurrection, Christ has secured the grace by which we are saved, as further attested in Ephesians 2:8-9,

> *"For by grace you have been saved through faith, and that not of yourselves; it is the gift of God, not of works, lest anyone should boast."*

Galatians 3:13 references the Old Testament law:

*"Cursed is everyone who hangs on a tree."*

Paul explains that Christ became a curse for us by being crucified (giving His Life for our), thereby redeeming us from the curse of the law. Similarly, Titus 2:14 speaks of Christ who

> *"gave himself for us, that he might redeem us from all iniquity, and purify unto himself a peculiar people, zealous of good works."*

Collectively, these passages bear witness to the truth that through His death, burial, and resurrection, Jesus fulfilled the role of the kinsman-redeemer, paying the ultimate price to liberate humanity from sin and its consequences, and effecting reconciliation between God and humankind.

## Jesus as "Savior."

When considering the person and work of Jesus Christ as Savior, it becomes evident that both the Old and New Testaments present abundant testimony to the divinely ordained purpose of His incarnation and redemptive mission. The sacred Scriptures, from Genesis to Revelation, consistently affirm God's sovereign plan to send His Son into the world for the salvation of humankind. In this, those who accept Christ allow God to showcase His love, mercy, grace, forgiveness, and righteousness to the world and all creation. Those who reject Christ will experience the wrath of God (the lake of fire), prepared for Satan, his demons, and the children of disobedience, for all eternity (the ages to come). Within the unity of the Godhead, Father, Son, and Holy Spirit, Jesus Christ is revealed as the Creator, through whom and for whom all things were made. The eternal counsel of the Triune God established from before the foundation of the world that redemption would be accomplished through Christ, who is the cornerstone of salvation for all humanity.

Let us, therefore, consider several key passages from both the Old and New Testaments that illuminate the reality of grace manifested through Jesus Christ, the Savior of the world. In Isaiah 43:3, the Lord proclaims,

> *"For I am the Lord your God, The Holy One of Israel, your Savior;" (NKJV).*

Here, the Lord identifies Himself as the eternal "I Am," the self-existent One, a designation later revealed in the person of Jesus Christ, who was with the Father from the beginning and is Himself the incarnate Word of God. Also, in this verse, the Word, who is Jesus Christ, God's only begotten Son, tells us that he is our saviour and the Holy One of Israel. The New Testament further clarifies this saving purpose. In Matthew 1:21, the angel declares,

> *"And she will bring forth a Son, and you shall call His name Jesus, for He will save His people from their sins." (NKJV).*

God sent an angel to Joseph in a dream, instructing him not to fear taking Mary as his wife, since what is conceived in her is of the Holy Spirit. Mary will bear a son, and Joseph is to name him Jesus, for He will save His people from their sins. Likewise, Luke 2:11 proclaim the birth of the Savior:

*"For there is born to you this day in the city of David a Savior, who is Christ the Lord." (NKJV).*

Other passages reinforce this truth, such as Acts 4:12, which asserts that salvation is found in no one else but Christ, and 1 John 4:14, which testifies,

*"And we have seen and do testify that the Father sent the Son to be the Saviour of the world" (KJV).*

As believers, we join in this testimony, bearing witness that Jesus Christ is indeed the Savior, the Son of God, sent by the Father for the redemption of all who believe.

## Jesus as the Son of God

To attain a deeper understanding of Jesus as the Son of God, it is fitting to begin with the prophetic writings of the Old Testament. The prophet Isaiah, in Chapter 9, Verse 6, proclaims:

*"For unto us a child is born, unto us a son is given: and the government shall be upon his shoulder: and his name shall be called Wonderful, Counsellor, The mighty God, The everlasting Father, The Prince of Peace." (King James Version)*

Here, Isaiah foretells the advent of a child who is to be given to humanity (all mankind), upon whose shoulders authority shall rest. The titles ascribed to this child, including "The mighty God," testify to the divine nature of

41

the One identified as the Son, thus affirming His unique relationship as the Son of God. The title "The everlasting Father" signifies Christ's relationship as the Son of God and identifies Him as the Spoken Word of God the Father. Numerous passages of Scripture further attest to Jesus' identity as the Son of God. The Gospel of John, Chapter 1, Verse 14 (Amplified Bible), declares:

> *"And the Word (Christ) became flesh, and lived among us; and we [actually] saw His glory, glory as belongs to the [One and] only begotten Son of the Father, [the Son who is truly unique, the only One of His kind, who is] full of grace and truth (absolutely free of deception)."*

In this passage, it is revealed that the eternal Word of God took on human flesh and dwelt among us, manifesting the glory unique to the only begotten Son of the Father. He is full of grace and truth, embodying the very essence of divine favor and veracity, sent so that through Him, salvation might be granted to the world.

Furthermore, the divine testimony concerning Jesus is expressly articulated in the account of His baptism. The Gospel according to Matthew, Chapter 3, Verses 16–17 (King James Version), records:

> *"And Jesus, when he was baptized, went up straightway out of the water: and, lo, the heavens were opened unto him, and he saw the Spirit of God descending like a dove, and lighting upon him: and lo a voice from heaven, saying, This is my beloved Son, in*

*whom I am well pleased."*

Here, the Father's own voice affirms Jesus' unique son-ship, placing His divine approval and endorsement upon Him as His beloved Son. This truth is further echoed in John 3:16, wherein it is declared:

*"For God so loved the world, that he gave his only begotten Son, that whosoever believeth in him should not perish, but have everlasting life."*

Such passages manifest the immeasurable and unconditional love of God, who, in giving His only begotten Son, provides the means by which all who believe may receive eternal life through Jesus Christ. In conclusion to this chapter, entitled "Grace Through Jesus Christ," we discern the presence of Christ manifested in manifold ways and throughout every dimension of our lives: in His nature, His character, and His boundless love. Every aspect of His divine being is revealed in the Holy Scriptures, wherein God presents His Son, Jesus Christ, and the grace by which we are granted salvation through Him, our Lord.

Therefore, let us endeavor to walk in a manner worthy of our calling, persevering in the Word of God, that we may ultimately partake of the prize, namely, the grace of God bestowed upon us through Jesus Christ. As we persist in our exploration of the profound doctrine of the Word of God, I earnestly exhort you, beloved in Christ, to remain steadfast in the reading of Holy Scripture, to meditate upon its precepts, to diligently study its depths, to offer prayers shaped by the very words of God to our Father in Heaven, and to faithfully apply its truths to the fabric of our daily existence. Through such devotion, we shall increasingly comprehend the magnitude and depth of God's boundless, unconditional love for humanity, a love most fully revealed in the sacrificial death of His Son.

Furthermore, we shall consider the means by which we are made partakers of the grace that alone brings salvation, a grace wrought through Jesus Christ our Lord, whereby we are delivered from the impending wrath reserved for the children of disobedience. Sin, in its essence, is missing the mark, a falling short of the glory of God; thus, recognizing our inherent inability to attain perfect righteousness, we acknowledge our profound need for a Savior, one who will lead us in conformity to the Word and will of God.

To this end, God in His infinite mercy sent His only begotten Son, Jesus Christ, to exemplify perfect obedience and to reveal the path by which we may return to fellowship with the Father, thereby receiving the gift of salvation through Him. Grace, being the unmerited favor of God, is not something we could ever merit or acquire by our own efforts. Yet, in His inscrutable wisdom and unwavering love for mankind, God graciously bestowed upon us the greatest gift the world has ever known, Jesus Christ, the incarnate Word of God. Thus, it is through Christ that we have access to grace, and in Him alone is our salvation secure. To God be the glory, both now and forevermore. Amen.

⟨ CHAPTER 3 ⟩

## JESUS PURPOSE FOR COMING

𝓗aving now grasped the nature of grace and its mediation through Jesus Christ, let us devote ourselves to a deeper contemplation of the divine purpose for our Lord's incarnation. Previously, we touched upon Adam's fall from grace, occasioned by his disobedience to God's explicit command: not to eat of the tree of the knowledge of good and evil. Yet, to attain a fuller understanding of Christ's redemptive mission, it is fitting that we examine more closely the account of Adam's transgression and its profound implications.

It was the Creator's original design that man should dwell eternally upon the earth, exercising dominion as the appointed steward over creation, just as God reigns sovereignty over the heavens and all that is spiritual. Jehovah, the Almighty, is the one true God, the Lord of heaven and earth, and of all that exists; there is none beside Him. Nevertheless, God fashioned Adam in His own image and likeness, endowing him with authority over all the works of His hands upon the earth.

Tragically, Adam violated the divine command and partook of the forbidden fruit, thus falling from the grace in which he had been established. In response to this act, and driven by His unfathomable love for humankind, God initiated His plan of redemption to restore fallen humanity to Himself. By Adam's disobedience came death, that is, separation from the life of God. As Scripture teaches, the consequences of Adam's sin extended to all his descendants, for in Adam all humanity shares both his fall and his mortality.

During Adam's reign, having been granted dominion over the works of God's hand and ordained by God, humanity possessed the authority, influence, and sovereign right to govern the earth as stewards. However, through Adam's disobedience, these dominion rights were forfeited, transferring control to Satan, who subsequently became the ruler of this world and its systems. As a result, Satan, whose sole purpose is to steal, kill, and destroy, now exerts influence, leading to chaos, calamity, and the proliferation of evil. Although God has declared Satan profane, rendering him useless, powerless, and without inherent authority, his works are nevertheless manifested through his influence over humanity. Satan and his demons, as disembodied spirits, lack the capacity to act in the physical world unless they deceive and persuade individuals to carry out their intentions, since all actions in the material realm require a physical body. Therefore, Adam's fall from grace resulted in the fall of all humanity.

Consequently, Adam's transgression resulted in a rupture of communion with Almighty God, a separation not only for himself but for all humanity who came after him. In order to restore humanity to Himself, it was necessary that an atonement be made for the sins of mankind, a task for which no ordinary man was sufficient, for humanity, rendered spiritually dead by sin, was incapable of effecting its own redemption. What was required to reconcile man to God was not to be found within the created order, for although it was through a living man that sin entered the world, no living man was found worthy to offer himself as a ransom for humanity, since all were subject to death and sin.

In His divine wisdom, therefore, God ordained to beget a Son, One who would be truly alive, wholly worthy, and perfectly obedient to every precept and commandment, pleasing God in all things. This Son would embody perfect righteousness and wisdom, fulfilling the law in its entirety and manifesting the fullness of sonship to God. Unlike Adam, who was formed directly by God and yet fell, this Redeemer would enter the world as all men do, being born of a woman, thus fully sharing in our humanity.

Thus, God prepared a body, for His eternal Word, by whom all things were made, and without whom nothing exists, became flesh. In the fullness of time, God brought forth His only begotten Son, and called His name Emmanuel, meaning 'God with us.' This is He whom we know as Jesus the Christ, the Savior of the world.

The incarnation of Jesus Christ was divinely purposed, and among the chief reasons for His coming to earth, I would highlight the following three, which will be further explored in this work:

➢ To fulfill the will of the Father who sent Him, by effecting the restoration of the relationship between God and mankind
➢ To seek and to save that which was lost, thereby delivering humanity from the bondage of sin
➢ To offer His life as a ransom for many through His sacrificial death, burial, and resurrection, thus bestowing the promise of eternal life

These foundational purposes form the heart of the redemptive mission of our Lord Jesus Christ.

Now, let us examine more closely the divine purposes for which Jesus Christ came into the world.

**To Fulfill the Father's Will**

As recorded in the Gospel according to John (6:38–40):

> *"For I have come down from heaven, not to do my own will but to do the will of him who sent me. And this is the will of him who sent me, that I should lose nothing of all that he has given me, but raise it up on the last day. For this is the will of my Father, that everyone who looks on the Son and believes in him should have eternal life, and I will raise him up on the last day."*

Here, our Lord explicitly affirms His heavenly origin and His singular devotion to accomplishing the will of the Father. Christ's mission was not self-initiated, but divinely commissioned; He came in obedience, endowed with the authority of the One who sent Him. The preservation and ultimate resurrection of all whom the Father has given to the Son is central to this divine purpose. The phrase "raise it up on the last day" alludes to the new creation, believers, made new through Christ, clothed in righteousness, and presented before God.

As the apostle Paul declares in 2 Corinthians 5:17,

> *"Therefore, if anyone is in Christ, he is a new*

*creation. The old has passed away; behold, the new has come." (ESV)*

Moreover, Jesus reiterates His divine commission in John 8:42:

*"Jesus said to them, 'If God were your Father, you would love me, for I came from God and I am here. I came not of my own accord, but he sent me.'" (ESV)*

To the Jewish audience, Jesus reveals that His presence and words are not self-derived, but proceed from the Father, underscoring both His divine origin and obedience to the Father.

## To Sacrifice Himself

In considering the purpose of Christ's incarnation, it is instructive to reflect upon the earliest biblical intimations of sacrifice and redemption. Immediately after the fall of humanity, Scripture records a significant event in Genesis 3:21:

*"And the Lord God made for Adam and for his wife garments of skins and clothed them" (ESV).*

The New Living Translation renders this verse,

*"And the Lord God made clothing from animal skins for Adam and his wife."*

Although the text does not explicitly mention a sacrifice, many theologians discern here an implied act of atonement, as the provision of animal skins necessarily presupposes the death of an animal. Thus, God's act may be interpreted as the first sacrifice, prefiguring the covering of human shame through the shedding of innocent blood, a motif that finds its ultimate fulfillment in the redemptive work of Christ.

The theme of sacrifice continues in Genesis 4, where Cain and Abel bring offerings to the Lord. Abel's offering,

*"the firstborn of his flock and of their fat portions,"*

is accepted, while Cain's offering from the fruit of the ground is not. The distinction is commonly understood to lie in the nature and quality of the sacrifices: Abel's gift entailed the shedding of innocent blood and was given in faith, whereas Cain's was deficient in devotion. This episode further anticipates the necessity of a substitutionary and acceptable sacrifice, a theme that echoes throughout the history of redemption.

A particularly profound foreshadowing occurs in the account of Abraham and Isaac (Genesis 22:6–19). At God's command, Abraham prepares to offer his beloved son Isaac as a burnt offering, only to be restrained by divine intervention. Instead, God provides a ram as a substitute, and Abraham names the place Jehovah Jireh,

*"The Lord Will Provide."*

The Lord's subsequent pronouncement,

*"and in your seed all the nations of the earth*

*shall be blessed, because you have obeyed My voice" (Genesis 22:18),*

is often understood as a prophetic reference to the coming Messiah. Thus, the binding of Isaac prefigures the sacrificial offering of Christ, the true Lamb of God, who would one day lay down His life to redeem humanity and take away the sins of the world.

Through these foundational narratives, Scripture progressively reveals the divine purpose for Christ's advent: to seek and to save the lost by offering Himself as the once-and-for-all sacrifice for sin, fulfilling the archetype established in the earliest chapters of Genesis and foreshadowed throughout the Old Testament.

## To Bring Abundant Life

In the Gospel according to John, our Lord contrasts His own purpose with that of the adversary:

*"The thief does not come except to steal, and to kill, and to destroy. I have come that they may have life, and that they may have it more abundantly." (John 10:10, NKJV).*

Jesus, the Son of God, offers not merely life, but life in its fullness, spiritual abundance, overflowing from His own divine sufficiency. In Him, believers find the true and everlasting life that God intends for His people. Together, these purposes reveal the fullness of Christ's mission: to fulfill the will of the Father, to save the lost, and to bestow abundant life upon all who believe. Theologically, the abundant life offered by Christ transcends mere biological existence; it encompasses spiritual regeneration, restoration, and the participation in the divine life, which is accessible solely through union with Him. Through His redemptive work, Christ exercises divine authority to bestow and restore life to those alienated from God.

The adversary, identified as Satan, whose singular intent is the spiritual deprivation, destruction, and ultimate ruin of humanity. The thief's activity is characterized by malice, stealing, killing, and destroying, reflecting his intrinsic opposition to God's purposes and benevolence.

Thus, all who respond in faith to Christ's call experience the realization of His salvific purpose and become recipients of God's gracious gift. His abundant life is not merely future-oriented but begins in the present, as believers are transformed by grace and brought into communion with God.

Let us consider the words of the Apostle John in Chapter 3, Verses 16-19 (KJV). These words convey a profound expression of God's love for humanity. There is more said here than anyone can imagine because the depth of God's love for mankind, the apple of His eye, and the Glory of the Father is found in these verses, and as we consider the words that have been spoken, let us remember that God's love is unconditional, and great is his love toward us. The scripture reads this way:

> *"For God so loved the world that He gave His only begotten Son, that whoever believes in Him should not perish but have everlasting life. For God did not send His Son into the world to condemn the world, but that the world through Him might be saved. He who*

*believes in Him is not condemned; but he who does not believe is condemned already, because he has not believed in the name of the only begotten Son of God. And this is the condemnation, that the light has come into the world, and men loved darkness rather than light, because their deeds were evil." John 3:16-19 (NKJV).*

Who better to explain the love of God than the one who loves Christ the most? John's love for Jesus was probably greater than that of any of Jesus' disciples during his earthly ministry. Jesus tells us in verse 16 that God's love for mankind was so great that when he fell from grace and died, men became worthy of death, and rightly so, they deserve to be punished, cast in the lake of fire, along with Satan and his demons, for whom the lake of fire was made. According to Isaiah 14:12-15 and Ezekiel 28:12-19, Lucifer brought sin into existence. In contrast, Genesis 3:1-20 states that Adam brought sin into the world and the domain of mankind through his disobedience.

This has now become man's fate after the fall, due to his disobedience, but God's love for man is so great that He decided to give man a second chance at life. Man was God's child through creation because we were all created in God's image and after his likeness. Man was created in a special way, which we will discuss in a later chapter. According to John, God sent his [only begotten] son into the world, not to condemn the world because of what they had done and what they were doing, but that the world through him might be saved. This opportunity would give man a second chance at life and be safe from the wrath of God that is to come on Satan, his demon, and the children of disobedience. God's wrath is as terrible as his love is great. God's love is boundless, and so is his wrath.

The advent of Jesus Christ was divinely foreordained by God the Father for manifold purposes: to accomplish the perfect will of the One who sent Him, to seek and to save those who are lost, and to offer His life as a ransom for many. The magnitude of God's love for humanity surpasses all human comprehension; His ways are unsearchable, and the depth of His affection for mankind testifies to the unique dignity bestowed upon humanity as the crown of His creation. Such profound love is revealed supremely in the Father's willingness to sacrifice His only begotten Son to redeem a fallen race, those who, though created as children, had become estranged from grace and stood deserving of eternal separation from God.

Nevertheless, in the boundlessness of divine mercy, God has granted humanity a second opportunity for life through Jesus Christ our Lord. Thus, the redemptive mission of Christ directly concerns every individual, for in Him we are restored to our original purpose: to become children of the Most High, holy, righteous, and conformed to all that is good. This is our created destiny and vocation.

Consequently, each person is confronted with a decisive choice: whether to embrace communion with God or to remain in alienation, facing the prospect of eternal separation. May all glory be ascribed to God, now and forever! Amen.

## A Unique Relationship
John tells us that God gave his only begotten son. What does this word begotten mean in the biblical sense,

and what does it mean in reference to God and his son, Jesus Christ? In the biblical sense, the word "begotten" refers to the relationship between a parent and their offspring, or child. The word "begotten," as it relates to God and His Son, Jesus, signifies a unique relationship between the Father and the Son. Jesus is God's only begotten son, and this is what makes the relationship unique.

Now, let us take a look at Psalm Eight. The scripture reads like this,

*"O Lord, our Lord, How excellent is Your name in all the earth, Who have set Your glory above the heavens! Out of the mouth of babes and nursing infants You have ordained strength, Because of Your enemies, That You may silence the enemy and the avenger. When I consider Your heavens, the work of Your fingers, The moon and the stars, which You have ordained, What is man that You are mindful of him, And the son of man that You visit him? For You have made him a little lower than the angels, And You have crowned him with glory and honor. You have made him to have dominion over the works of Your hands; You have put all things under his feet, All sheep and oxen—Even the beasts of the field, The birds of the air, And the fish of the sea That pass through the paths of the seas. O Lord, our Lord, How excellent is Your name in all the earth!" Psalm 8:1-9 KJV*

The psalms also tell us of the uniqueness not just of

God's Son, Jesus, but that of humanity as well. Mankind, except for Adam and Eve, is also a begotten being by their parents, which makes us a unique being to our parents. Yes, we are unique to our parents and ancestors, and we could have only come through them. Let us consider Psalms Chapter 8, Verses 4 and 5. Listen to what is being said here. The scriptures read this way,

> *"What is man that You are mindful of him, And the son of man that You visit him? For You have made him a little lower than the angels, And You have crowned him with glory and honor." Psalm 8:4-5 (NKJV).*

The Psalmist poses a profound question about the importance of humanity and the attention God gives to it. Remember, in the Garden of Eden, God frequently visited Adam and his wife. The Bible doesn't specify how often, but we do know that God visited Adam and Eve in the Garden of Eden. The scriptures go on to tell us that man was made a little lower than the angels. The word "angels" here refers to the Hebrew word Elohim, which is the same word used for God in Hebrew at the beginning of the book of Genesis. The Hebrew term 'Elohim' signifies the concept of three-in-one, referring to the Holy Trinity: Father, Son, and Holy Spirit. Here, the psalmist tells us that man was made a little lower than God, not angels. The psalmist also tells us that man was crowned with Glory and Honor. This, I believe, is a direct reference to the Lord Jesus Christ, for his triumph over death, burial, and resurrection as the Son of God.

The relationship between Jesus and the Father is unique. Prior to the fullness of time, Jesus existed as the spoken and written Word of God, present with God throughout eternity past, present, and future. With the arrival of the fullness of time, Jesus, the Word of God, became the only begotten or unique Son of God. This relationship encompasses both spiritual and physical dimensions, establishing Jesus as the sole begotten and unique Son of God the Father.

## To Seek and Save the Lost

The Lord Himself proclaims in Luke 19:9-10 (KJV), as the scripture records:

> *"And Jesus said unto him, This day is salvation come to this house, forsomuch as he also is a son of Abraham. For the Son of man is come to seek and to save that which was lost."*

And in 1 Timothy 1:15, the apostle Paul further testifies,

> *"Christ Jesus came into the world to save sinners."*

The redemptive mission of Christ, to seek out and redeem those estranged from God, stands at the heart of His earthly ministry. This divine intervention is of profound significance, as it addresses the essential need of humanity, which is that of fallen creatures in need of salvation.

This pericope recounts Jesus' encounter with Zacchaeus, a chief tax collector of Jericho, whose wealth and diminutive stature did not preclude his earnest desire to behold the Lord. In an act of humility and anticipation, Zacchaeus climbed a sycamore tree to catch a glimpse of

Jesus as He passed by. Recognizing both Zacchaeus's faith and his longing for redemption, Jesus called him down and declared His intention to abide in his house that day, an act met with murmurs from the crowd, who objected to Jesus' association with a reputed sinner.

Within Zacchaeus's home, Christ's ministry prompted a profound transformation: Zacchaeus vowed to give half his possessions to the poor and to restore fourfold any fraudulent gain. In response, Jesus affirmed that salvation had come to Zacchaeus's house, explicitly identifying him as a true son of Abraham, thereby underscoring the inclusivity of God's redemptive purpose. Jesus then articulated the heart of His mission:

*"For the Son of Man came to seek and to save the lost."*

This narrative exemplifies the universal scope of Christ's salvific work. Theologically, it manifests the initiative of divine grace, whereby the incarnate Son pursues those estranged from God through sin. As echoed in 1 Timothy 1:15,

*"Christ Jesus came into the world to save sinners."*

The apostolic witness affirms the redemptive intent of the incarnation. Moreover, the process of salvation is not merely forensic but transformative; as believers engage with Scripture through reading, meditation, prayer, and daily application, the Holy Spirit reveals the mysteries of God's truth, which were previously concealed from the world but are now revealed to the faithful. Thus, salvation encompasses both the objective work of Christ and the subjective illumination and renewal wrought by the Spirit in the believer's life.

In conclusion, Jesus' purpose for entering the world was, and remains, to fulfill the will of His Heavenly Father by seeking and saving the lost and offering His life as a ransom for many. The work of Jesus, ordained by the Father, was to reconcile and restore to God that which is most precious to Him: humanity, the crown of His creation, created in the divine image and likeness. The depth of God's love for humanity is demonstrated in His willingness to restore those separated from Him through disobedience and to grant eternal life through His Son, Jesus Christ, as an expression of divine grace.

〈 CHAPTER 4 〉

## THE SAVING GRACE OF GOD

Jn our previous discussions, we have examined the multifaceted nature of grace, considering both its various forms and the manifold ways in which individuals may encounter it throughout their lives. We have sought to define grace itself, explored its manifestation through Jesus Christ, and reflected on the redemptive purpose of Christ's incarnation. At this juncture, an essential question arises: Do we truly comprehend the nature and significance of the saving grace of God? To address this, let us briefly revisit our foundational understanding of grace. As established in Chapter 1, "What Is Grace," grace, in theological terms, signifies the freely bestowed, unmerited favor and love of God. The term "unmerited" denotes that this favor is neither earned nor deserved by human effort. Thus, the inquiry before us, "what is the saving grace of God?" demands careful consideration.

To elucidate this concept, consider that even if one possessed all the wealth of the universe, its aggregate value being beyond calculation or imagination, it would remain wholly insufficient to redeem a single soul, let alone the multitude of souls that have ever lived or will ever exist. The reason for this ineffable value lies in the creation narrative: when God breathed into Adam's nostrils the breath of life, He imparted a portion of His own Spirit. From this divine breath sprang human life, and man became a living soul, thus endowing each person with immeasurable worth.

However, as a consequence of the fall in the Garden of Eden, humanity became estranged from God; spiritually dead, though physically alive, owing to Adam's transgression. Because of this disobedience, we are justly deserving of death rather than life. Our separation from God renders us incapable, utterly unable, to pay the penalty for our sins or to secure our own salvation. The price of redemption is incalculably great; it surpasses all earthly riches. Therefore, there is nothing we can do to merit or attain salvation by our own means.

Accordingly, only God can provide the means of salvation, accomplishing for us what we ourselves are powerless to achieve. This He has done through the Word made flesh, our Creator, the Lord Jesus Christ, who alone is our Redeemer and Savior. With this truth in mind, let us turn to the Holy Scriptures to further illuminate the doctrine of saving grace. We begin with the Apostle Paul's words in Ephesians 2:4–10 (NKJV):

> *"But God, who is rich in mercy, because of His great love with which He loved us, even when we were dead in trespasses, made us alive together with Christ (by grace you have been saved), and raised us up together, and made us sit together in the heavenly places in Christ Jesus, that in the ages to come He might show the exceeding riches of His grace in His kindness toward us in Christ Jesus. For by grace you have been saved through faith, and that not of yourselves; it is the gift of God, not of works, lest anyone should boast. For we are His workmanship, created in Christ Jesus for good works, which God prepared beforehand*

*that we should walk in them."*

God, who is Jehovah Jireh, the Lord our Provider, is inexhaustible in His resources; He possesses an infinite sufficiency and is ever able to supply the needs of His people. As the Apostle Paul affirms in Philippians 4:19 (KJV):

> *"But my God shall supply all your need according to his riches in glory by Christ Jesus."*

The abundance of God is not limited, nor can it ever be depleted, for His provision flows from the richness of His glory through Christ.

Moreover, as Paul begins his discourse in Ephesians, he proclaims the superabundance of God's mercy and the greatness of His love toward us. Even when we were spiritually dead in our trespasses, God, in His grace, made us alive together with Christ Jesus. How marvelous is the love of our holy and righteous Lord, who, though we were sinners deserving of death, bestowed upon us the gift of life in Christ! Indeed, as it is written in Romans 9:15, the Lord declares to Moses:

> *"...I will have mercy on whom I will have mercy, and I will have compassion on whom I will have compassion."*

Thus, the riches of God's mercy and compassion are manifest to us. Paul further elucidates in Ephesians 2:5–6 that even while we were dead in our sins, God quickened us together with Christ, saved us by grace, raised us up with

Him, and seated us in heavenly places in Christ Jesus, all because of His abundant mercy and great love.

Furthermore, as Romans 8:14 (KJV) proclaims:

*"For as many as are led by the Spirit of God, they are the sons of God."*

It is a profound privilege to be granted wisdom, knowledge, and understanding by God, granting us insight into His Word. As believers and followers of our Lord Jesus Christ, we recognize that all we are and all we accomplish are in and through Christ. Apart from Him, we can do nothing, for He is the Way, the Truth, and the Life; in Him we live, move, and have our being. Separated from Christ, we remain spiritually dead, estranged from God.

Yet, in His manifold mercy, God has bestowed upon us the supreme gift of life through Jesus Christ. Because of Christ's redemptive work, we who were once dead in our trespasses and sins have now been made alive in Him. Only in Christ is true life found, for the Father has given to the Son not only the authority to create life but also to impart it. Thus, through union with Jesus Christ, we are restored to life and fellowship with God.

As children of God, born of His Spirit, cleansed by the blood of Jesus, and made the righteousness of God in Christ, we stand justified not by our own merit, but by faith in God the Father and His only begotten Son. It is by this faith that we have received the incomparable gift of God's grace, which delivers us from the wrath to come upon the world and the children of disobedience. Accordingly, we affirm that our God abounds in grace, mercy, love, and kindness, all that is good emanates from Him, who is immeasurably rich in every virtue, surpassing all human comprehension.

Permit me, then, to take a brief excursus to further elucidate the nature of saving grace by reflecting on the condition of humankind. Many remain unaware of their true identity, their purpose in life, or the reason for their existence. The answers to these existential questions are found in the Word of God, for Jesus is the Word made flesh, and thus, He Himself is the answer. He knows our needs before we perceive them, for the Scriptures declare that God discerns even the thoughts and intentions of the heart. Such is the omniscience and power of our God.

Therefore, as human beings, it is incumbent upon us first to seek a true knowledge of ourselves; the most effective means of attaining true understanding is through the Word of God. Just as one seeking to comprehend the nature and operation of a product consults its manufacturer and studies the accompanying manual, so too must we turn to our Creator, who alone possesses the blueprint for humanity and all creation. By engaging with the Scriptures, we receive divine revelation concerning our origin, purpose, and identity.

Therefore, it is imperative that we consult the Word of God in order to apprehend who we truly are. Then, we should inquire of God concerning our purpose, and ultimately to discern His will for our lives. In every matter, we ought to seek divine guidance, for, as the Psalmist declares, we are *"fearfully and wonderfully made:" Psalm 139:14.* Among all creation, humanity occupies a singular position, endowed with remarkable capabilities by virtue of being created in the image and likeness of God. Even in our fallen state, we have accomplished much, and greatness, a testament to the Creator's design.

Grace, theologically understood, is the freely given, unmerited favor and love of God, unmerited, in that it cannot be earned or deserved by any human effort. The Apostle Paul declares in Ephesians 2:8:

> *"For by grace you have been saved through faith, and that not of yourselves; it is the gift of God..."*

Salvation, then, is not a reward for human achievement but a gift bestowed purely out of divine love.

What does it mean to be saved by grace through faith? Grace is a gift given freely, apart from merit or recompense, and beyond the ability of fallen humanity to procure. While material things may be obtained through human endeavor, spiritual salvation remains utterly unattainable apart from divine intervention. This grace becomes accessible to us through faith in Jesus Christ: when we confess with our mouths that Jesus is Lord and believe in our hearts that He is the Son of God, was crucified, buried, and raised from the dead for our justification, then by His grace, a free gift, the unmerited favor of God, we are saved.

This exercise of faith is pleasing to God the Father, for in acknowledging and receiving His Son, Jesus Christ, we are granted the gift of grace that affects our salvation through faith in Him. The magnitude of salvation is such that no human effort or labor, even extended through eternity, could ever suffice to secure or merit it; its value surpasses all conceivable means. Thus, salvation is not earned, it is bestowed. God grants this gift solely on account of faith, not as a result of human accomplishment, but as a manifestation of His own benevolent purpose accomplished in Christ Jesus. All glory and thanksgiving belong to God for the inestimable gift He has given us in His Son. As the Apostle Paul affirms,

> *"it is not by works, so that no one may boast; for we are his workmanship, created in Christ Jesus" (cf. Ephesians 2:9-10).*

Nevertheless, the saving grace of God is His free gift, not because we are worthy or capable of attaining it ourselves, but precisely because we must confess our need for a Savior, and that Savior is Jesus Christ. God sent His Son into the world to redeem humanity from sin, for we are powerless to save ourselves. Christ, therefore, is the supreme manifestation of God's grace to humankind. Scripture assures us that ***if we confess our sins, God is faithful and just to forgive us and to cleanse us from all unrighteousness (cf. 1 John 1:9).*** The Apostle Paul further elucidates in Romans 10:9-10 (CSB):

> *"If you confess with your mouth, 'Jesus is Lord,' and believe in your heart that God raised him from the dead, you will be saved. One believes with the heart, resulting in righteousness, and one confesses with the mouth, resulting in salvation."*

Thus, we affirm that salvation comes as we openly confess Jesus as the Son of God, who was, crucified, buried, and rose on the third day, and believe in the testimony of Scripture. Our faith rests upon the Word of God, which assures us of the redemptive work of Christ. By this faith, we are saved by grace. Moreover, the writer to the Hebrews declares:

> *"But without faith it is impossible to please Him, for he who comes to God must believe that He is, and that He is a rewarder of those who diligently seek Him." (Hebrews 11:6, KJV).*

Let us briefly reflect upon this profound truth: to approach God acceptably requires faith, both in His existence and in His gracious disposition to reward those who earnestly seek Him. The conjunction "and" in this verse is of great significance, indicating that both beliefs are indispensable, one must believe both that God is, and that He rewards the diligent seeker. The implication is clear: faith in God must be rooted in the revelation of His Word, for it is in the Scriptures that God makes Himself known.

God is not to be found merely in familial ties, social relationships, worldly systems, or the opinions of others. While the testimonies of fellow believers may edify, genuine faith is born and sustained by engagement with the living Word of God. As Paul teaches, ***"faith comes by hearing, and hearing by the word of God"*** (Romans 10:17). He likewise exhorts Timothy,

> *"Study to shew thyself approved unto God, a workman that needeth not to be ashamed, rightly dividing the word of truth" (2 Timothy 2:15, KJV).*

The New King James Version reads this way:

*"Be diligent to present yourself approved to God, a worker who does not need to be ashamed, rightly dividing the word of truth."*

Therefore, let us diligently seek God in His Word, that our faith may be strengthened, our understanding deepened, and our lives conformed to His will by the grace so freely given in Christ Jesus.

Let us now address the question: What is meant by the saving grace of God? To facilitate a deeper understanding of this profound theological concept, it is essential to state succinctly that the answer is found in the person of Jesus Christ. To apprehend the significance of His salvific work, one must return to the very inception of creation. God, in His sovereign will and for His ultimate purpose and pleasure, brought into existence the heavens and the earth and all that inhabits them. Among His creations was Adam, whose name signifies man, mankind, or humanity, and to whom God granted dominion over the whole earth.

The Lord God established a garden eastward in Eden, a dwelling place for Adam, abounding with trees that were both pleasing to the eye and good for food. In the midst of this garden, God planted two trees of particular significance: the tree of life, intended for humanity, and the tree of the knowledge of good and evil, reserved for Himself.

The fruits of the tree of life imparted sustenance and

vitality to the physical body. This is attested in the Holy Scriptures, specifically Genesis 3:22-24 (KJV):

*"And the LORD God said, Behold, the man is become as one of us, to know good and evil: and now, lest he put forth his hand, and take also of the tree of life, and eat, and live for ever: therefore the LORD God sent him forth from the garden of Eden, to till the ground from whence he was taken. So he drove out the man; and he placed at the east of the garden of Eden Cherubims, and a flaming sword which turned every way, to keep the way of the tree of life."*

The Amplified Bible renders these verses thus:

*"And the Lord God said, 'Behold, the man has become like one of Us (Father, Son, Holy Spirit), knowing [how to distinguish between] good and evil; and now, he might stretch out his hand, and take from the tree of life as well, and eat [its fruit], and live [in this fallen, sinful condition] forever'—therefore the Lord God sent Adam away from the Garden of Eden, to till and cultivate the ground from which he was taken. So God drove the man out; and at the east of the Garden of Eden He [permanently] stationed the cherubim and the sword with the flashing blade which turned round and round [in every direction] to protect and guard the way (entrance, access) to the tree of life. [Rev 2:7; 22:2, 14, 19] Genesis 3:22-24 (AMP)."*

The tree of the knowledge of good and evil constitutes the second tree that God planted in the midst of the Garden. This tree, unique in its purpose, imparts to those who partake of it both the awareness and the capacity to discern between good and evil. To Adam, the Lord God issued a solemn command:

> *"Of every tree of the garden you may freely eat; but of the tree of the knowledge of good and evil you shall not eat, for in the day that you eat of it you shall surely die." (Genesis 2:16–17, NKJV)*

Nevertheless, Adam transgressed the divine mandate and partook of the fruit of the tree of the knowledge of good and evil. By this act of disobedience, the curse of the fall befell humanity; sin thus entered the world, and the domain of man was fundamentally altered. It is crucial to recognize that this was not God's intention for humanity. God did not ordain that man should experience both good and evil, but rather only good, that he might reflect the image and likeness of his Creator.

In response to the fall, God enacted His preordained plan of redemption, for He, in His omniscience, foresaw man's disobedience. God's redemptive purpose was not to create another son from the dust, as He had with Adam, but to beget a Son in the fullness of humanity, one who would justify all who believe in Him and affirm His divine sonship.

Thus, God sent forth His Word, the Creator of all things, into the world. This Word was named Jesus, meaning "Savior", and Emmanuel, meaning "God with us." Born of a virgin, yet begotten by the Father, this miracle was accomplished when God dispatched the angel Gabriel to Mary, a virgin betrothed to Joseph of the house of David. Gabriel announced to Mary that she would conceive and bear a son, to be called Emmanuel. Questioning how this could be, since she knew no man, Mary received Gabriel's assurance of divine intervention, and by her faith, the Immaculate Conception was wrought within her.

In the fullness of time, Mary gave birth to her firstborn Son, naming Him Jesus. This Jesus is the Father's supreme gift to humankind, God's grace incarnate, so that all who believe in Him, acknowledging His divine sonship, His death, burial, and resurrection, shall receive salvation and the promise of eternal life.

Adam, notwithstanding the divine injunction, transgressed the explicit command of God and partook, together with Eve his wife, of the fruit of the tree of the knowledge of good and evil. This act precipitated the curse of the Fall, thereby opening the door for sin to enter the world, the very domain entrusted to mankind. Through Adam's disobedience, humanity was plunged into spiritual darkness, extinguishing the light that once illuminated the path of life. In this act, Adam subjected all of humanity to bondage, ushering calamity, chaos, and destruction into a world originally fashioned for God's good pleasure and the enjoyment of His creation. Thus, the disobedience of Adam resulted in the universal fall of mankind into sin.

However, Jesus Christ, the begotten Son of God would bestow eternal life upon mankind, in stark contrast to the first man, whose disobedience brought death. Thus,

God's plan to prepare a body for His living Word, sent forth His Word into the world, the Creator of all things, for the salvation of humanity, naming Him Jesus (Savior), born of a Virgin and conceived by the Holy Spirit. This Jesus is the Father's supreme gift to mankind, the incarnate Word, the Light of the world, the manifestation of divine grace, so that whoever believes in Him, shall receive salvation and eternal life. Such is the essence of 'The Saving Grace of God,' as affirmed in Acts 16:31 (KJV):

*"Believe on the Lord Jesus Christ, and thou shalt be saved, and thy house."*

Therefore, the ultimate question remains: How does one obtain this saving grace of God? Do you know?

‹ CHAPTER 5 ›

# HOW TO RECEIVE GOD SAVING GRACE

ℒet us now recapitulate the foundational themes explored in the preceding four chapters of this work: namely, "What is Grace," "Grace Through Jesus Christ," "Jesus Purpose for Coming," and "The Saving Grace of God." As we arrive at this culminating chapter, "How to Receive God Saving Grace," it becomes evident that this subject is of utmost significance, both within the context of this book and in the life of every believer. This chapter seeks to address the pivotal question that has the power to deliver individuals from the bondage of sin and the enslavement imposed by humanity's fallen state.

One may be inclined to assert that he or she is neither a slave nor held captive, believing themselves to be truly free. Yet, the truth revealed in Scripture is that apart from Christ and the regenerating work of the Holy Spirit, all are, in fact, enslaved to sin, held captive by its deception, and often unaware of their bondage, destined, unless redeemed, to experience the coming wrath reserved for the children of disobedience. How grievous will be that great and dreadful day when many will finally perceive that they have been deceived and held in bondage by spiritual forces, by Satan and his demonic hosts, who have led them astray from the truth that is found in Christ Jesus. As the Apostle Paul exhorts in 2 Corinthians 6:1-2 (NKJV):

> *"We then, as workers together with Him also plead with you not to receive the grace of God*

*in vain. For He says: 'In an acceptable time I have heard you, And in the day of salvation I have helped you.' Behold, now is the accepted time; behold, now is the day of salvation."*

From a theological perspective, grace is properly understood as God's unmerited favor, His gratuitous love extended to humanity. It is a gift freely given, for we neither merit it nor can we earn it. Yet, in His boundless love, God has bestowed this gift upon all who believe in His only begotten Son, Jesus Christ, as attested by the witness of The Holy Scripture, the Gospel, The Word of God, wherein it is written that whosoever believes shall be saved. In the Gospel according to John 3:16-18 (KJV), we read:

*"For God so loved the world, that he gave his only begotten Son, that whosoever believeth in him should not perish, but have everlasting life. For God sent not his Son into the world to condemn the world; but that the world through him might be saved. He that believeth on him is not condemned: but he that believeth not is condemned already, because he hath not believed in the name of the only begotten Son of God."*

Furthermore, if one confesses faith in the death, burial, and resurrection of Jesus Christ, as articulated by the Apostle Paul in 1 Corinthians 15:1-4 (KJV), it is written:

*"Moreover, brethren, I declare unto you the gospel which I preached unto you, which also*

*ye have received, and wherein ye stand; by which also ye are saved, if ye keep in memory what I preached unto you, unless ye have believed in vain. For I delivered unto you first of all that which I also received, how that Christ died for our sins according to the scriptures; and that he was buried, and that he rose again the third day according to the scriptures:"*

Thus, from the foregoing chapters, we have discerned the nature of grace, the means by which it is imparted through Jesus Christ, the redemptive purpose of His incarnation, and the saving grace of God that stands ready to redeem all who desire salvation.

But, before we proceed to address the central question, "How to Receive God Saving Grace," I would like to relate a personal testimony, an account that, I believe, vividly illustrates the superabundance of God's grace as revealed to me through the study and illumination of the Holy Scriptures. So, permit me to share this testimony of one of the manifold grace of God as manifested in my own life. The occasion to which I refer stands as a profound instance of divine revelation through the Holy Scriptures, wherein the Lord graciously imparted understanding and unveiled to me the true nature of our Lord Jesus Christ.

In the earliest days of my Christian pilgrimage and communion with God, I sought the guidance of my pastor, the late Bishop H. H. Allen, esteemed shepherd of the First Church of Christ Disciples in Jamaica, Queens, New York. Desiring to deepen my understanding of the sacred mysteries, I approached Bishop Allen with pressing inquiries concerning the faith, and he kindly consented to instruct me in the Scriptures.

At that time, I was a member of Bishop Allen's congregation, a Pentecostal assembly in Queens, New York, earnestly seeking to know the Lord Jesus Christ and to apprehend the triune God, Father, Son, and Holy Spirit, for myself. Though I had been raised in the church, true knowledge of God eluded me; I possessed only that which had been handed down to me by others. On that particular day, Pastor Allen and I devoted ourselves to studying the Gospel of John, Chapter One.

Several months prior to this pivotal encounter, I was profoundly impressed by the voice of the Holy Spirit, who spoke unto me, instructing: *"Take your Bible and a Dictionary, and every word you do not know, look it up and learn its meaning."* In humility, I responded to the Lord, confessing, 'You know, I cannot read, spell, or write, so how will I know what I am reading and what it means?' At that time, I struggled even to pronounce the simplest of words.

Yet, the Spirit of God, in His patience and mercy, reiterated the command: **Take your Bible and a Dictionary, and every word you do not know, look it up and learn its meaning.** On this occasion, however, the divine admonition was accompanied by further instruction: *"Listen to people's sentence structure."* Until then, I had no knowledge that sentences are governed by structure; yet I soon discerned that both speech and writing are to be governed by the proper use of the parts of speech, namely, nouns, pronouns, adjectives, verbs, adverbs, prepositions, conjunctions, and interjections.

At that juncture, I was in the midst of my twenties, possessing a reading ability scarcely above the elementary level. My capacity to read was, by all accounts, quite limited. At that moment, Pastor Allen endeavored to elucidate the profound truth that the Word of God is, indeed, Jesus Christ our Lord. Yet, despite his earnest explanations, his words eluded my comprehension; I was utterly unable to grasp the reality he sought to convey, and a growing sense of frustration took hold of me.

After approximately thirty minutes of earnest instruction, an extraordinary event transpired. The Holy Spirit graciously opened the eyes of my understanding and bestowed upon me divine revelation. It was as though the veil had been lifted from my mind, and a flood of understanding was poured into my soul. In that instant, the truth became unmistakably clear: I knew, beyond any shadow of doubt, that Jesus is the very Word of God. What a wondrous clarity the Lord imparted! The reality of the Word was made as plain to me as the light of day. Overwhelmed by the magnitude of this revelation, I could do nothing but weep for joy, my heart overflowing with gratitude and praise to God.

It was through the diligent reading of Holy Scripture that the Lord Jesus Himself became my instructor, teaching me to read by means of His Word. Thereafter, God began to commune with me through the sacred text, and I witnessed the living Word of God unfolding before my eyes. The Scriptures, once veiled in obscurity, became radiant with clarity, and the Lord graciously imparted to me wisdom, knowledge, understanding, and revelations concerning His Word. As it is written in Psalm 119:130:

> *"The entrance of thy words giveth light; it giveth understanding unto the simple." (King James Version)*

Psalm 119:130 of the New King James Version reads like this,

> *"The entrance of Your words gives light; It gives understanding to the simple."*

And the Amplified Bible of Psalm 119:130 reads this way,

> *"The unfolding of Your [glorious] words give light; Their unfolding gives understanding to the simple (childlike)."*

Such is the nature of grace: wholly undeserved and unmerited, yet bestowed by God, who is abundant in mercy and whose love toward us knows no condition. The Lord, in His infinite kindness, has instructed me in the reading of His Word that I might come to know Him through the power of His resurrection and the truth revealed in Holy Scripture.

It is through this wondrous grace that I received revelation and understanding concerning what I have come to regard as *"The Creation of Man."* This understanding of man's creation will help shed some glorious light on the reason for the saving grace of God. When considering how someone receives God's saving grace, a common question should arise: What does that process actually involve? It begins with forming a relationship with Jesus Christ, an essential commitment for every believer. With that said, allow me if you will to relate yet another personal testimony of God's grace in my life, which I trust will bring you much joy.

About ten years into my walk with Christ, I gained important spiritual insights. One of my most influential teachers, besides my Pastor, was the late Dr. Roy Hicks, whose teachings had a profound impact on me. When he spoke, God's word became clearer and more meaningful. I especially remember his statement: **"God can do nothing less than perfect or perfection."** This shaped my perspective, helping me realize God's actions are always perfect. Further reflecting on Ezekiel 28:15, that Lucifer, who was created perfect, was perfect until iniquity was found in him, deepened my understanding still more. With that in mind, let's now read Ezekiel 28:14-18 (KJV):

> *"Thou art the anointed cherub that covereth; and I have set thee so: thou wast upon the holy mountain of God; thou hast walked up and down in the midst of the stones of fire. Thou wast perfect in thy ways from the day that thou wast created, till iniquity was found in thee. By the multitude of thy merchandise they have filled the midst of thee with violence, and thou hast sinned: therefore I will cast thee as profane out of the mountain of God: and I will destroy thee, O covering cherub, from the midst of the stones of fire. Thine heart was lifted up because of thy beauty, thou hast corrupted thy wisdom by reason of thy brightness: I will cast thee to the ground, I will lay thee before kings, that they*

THE SAVING GRACE OF GOD

*may behold thee. Thou hast defiled thy sanctuaries by the multitude of thine iniquities, by the iniquity of thy traffick; therefore will I bring forth a fire from the midst of thee, it shall devour thee, and I will bring thee to ashes upon the earth in the sight of all them that behold thee."*

Reading Ezekiel 28:15, I understood that although it refers specifically to Lucifer, it illustrates how angels, as spirit beings always before God, are created perfect. This passage led me to believe that all angels were created as perfect spirit beings.

Now, I have not read nor found in the Bible where it says that man was created perfect. I'm not saying that we were not; even though Jesus tells us in the Bible that we are to be perfect as our Father in heaven is perfect. The Bible tells us how man was created, and we can find this information in the book of Genesis. I'm only saying here what the word of God said when man was created. When we look in the book of Genesis, Chapter 1, Verses 4, 12, 18, 21, and 25, God said at the end of each day, after creating what He was to create on that day, "God saw that what He had created was good." Then, on the sixth day, God created man in his image and after his likeness. He set man over the works of his hand, over his creation on the earth. In verse 31, after He created man, the Bible states that God saw everything that He had made and it was "very good." So, the Bible tells us that man and all things natural or physical, including the universe, were created very good, not perfect.

This led me to think deeply about the meaning of

'very good' in Genesis. If God always does perfect work, why distinguish between 'perfect' and 'very good'? My questions to God about this difference opened the door for further understanding, especially after reflecting on Dr. Roy Hicks's statement that "God can do nothing less than perfect or perfection."

The Lord showed me that I was limiting Him by believing He could only do perfect things. Dr. Roy Hicks said God can do **nothing less than perfect. After considering that statement, I realized that if** God can do nothing less than perfect, with emphasis on 'less than,' it opens the question: Can God do greater than perfect? The answer is yes, because He is God. Believing that God can only do perfect things limit His ability. God can do anything good, holy, just, and righteous. We should not limit God, and yes, there are some things that God cannot do. He cannot lie, fail, or deny Himself, which scripture supports. I also believe He cannot do evil or wrong. Therefore, when I was thinking God can only do perfect things, I unknowingly limit Him. God can do greater than perfect, more than we can imagine. There is no limit on God's ability, as seen when the Lord asks Abraham in Genesis 18:14.

*"Is anything too hard for the Lord?"*

The Lord then led me to examine the meanings of "very" and "good" as well as "truly" and "worthy," but before I do that, let me explain: a synonym is a word that has the same or nearly the same meaning as another in the same language. Synonyms can help avoid repetition or redundancy, a concept taught in grade school and one I learned further as an author.

Now, the word **Very** means "in a high degree; extremely; exceedingly: true; genuine; worthy of being called such."

The word **Good** means "morally excellent; virtuous; righteous; pious: of high quality; excellent; honorable or worthy; in good standing:"

The word **Truly** means "in accordance with fact or truth; truthfully: legitimately; by right: really; genuinely; honestly: to the fullest extent or degree: to a great extent or degree:

The word **Worthy** means "having adequate or great merit, character, or value: a person of eminent worth, merit, or position:

After looking up the meanings of "very" and "good," God had me look up their synonyms. The words that stood out were "truly" and "worthy." Suddenly, it was as if a light switched on in my mind. I understood what God wanted me to see: that He made man very good, not perfect, like the angels, and this understanding was undeniable. Let me share with you what the Lord revealed to me.

God showed me that a strong synonym for truly is surely and very; a strong synonym for good is worthy; a strong synonym for worthy is good.

Now, after understanding the meanings of the words "very" and "good" and the synonyms associated with each, the Lord opened my understanding. He gave me insight, or a revelation, if you will, that changed everything by answering my question. Why were we, humans, not made perfect, but very good? I am going to share this knowledge with you. Most importantly, it will help us understand why our relationship with Jesus Christ is so vital to our salvation and the gift of grace that God has given to us, humanity. This is not a new doctrine or a foundation for doctrine. It is just an understanding of how and why we were created.

God showed me that everything He created on earth was created "very good", meaning truly worthy of its purpose. The central message is that God designed everything, from ants to humans, to fulfill specific roles as He intended. Take the ant, for example: its strength, farming abilities, communication, and unique traits reveal that it is truly worthy of being what God created it to be.

Take the birds that fly in the heavens. They have the ability to move, some at extraordinary speed and with great accuracy. Some can see great distances from the sky. For example, there are many species of birds. The penguin is the only bird that can swim, yet not fly. Owls can turn their heads almost 360 degrees, but they cannot move their eyes. Chickens produce over 200 distinct noises for communication. Each species of bird is different. Each one is designed by God to be "truly worthy" and to do and be what He made them.

Then there are salmon. Salmon are anadromous fish, which means they migrate from the ocean to freshwater rivers, returning to their birthplace to spawn. There are different species of salmon. Wild salmon have a keen sense of smell, and they can change color. They live in two distinct environments during their lives. Their early lives are spent in freshwater rivers and streams. Some move to the open ocean to grow and mature before returning to freshwater rivers and streams for spawning. After spawning, adult salmon typically die. They provide nutrients for the next generation in the ecosystem. Each species is unique, yet God designed and made them "truly worthy" to do and be what He created them to be.

This was just to name a few of God's creations and creatures on earth. All were created by God, worthy of the abilities He gave them to do the things they were created to do. Then we come to man. Man was created in God's image and after God's likeness. He was given the authority to have dominion over all of God's creation, the work of His hand, on earth. Man was created worthy by God to hold the position of ruling. He was given complete authority and dominion over the fish of the sea, the birds of the air, the cattle, the entire earth, and everything that creeps and crawls on earth, just as God rules in Heaven. Man was worthy of life, even eternal life, because God had breathed life into him. God did not create a spirit and put it in man. He breathed the breath of life into man's nostrils, a part of Himself, and the man became a living soul. This man was worthy of God breathing life into him and giving him authority over the work of His hand.

What greater worthiness is there than to be created worthy by God for what He created us to be? Because we were created worthy by God, we have a tremendous responsibility. We are created in God's image and worthy of God's likeness. No other of God's creations is like man, not even the angels that stand in God's presence. But then something happened to mankind. Adam was commanded by God not to eat from the tree of the knowledge of good and evil, which God had planted in the center of the Garden of Eden. He could eat the fruit of all other trees except that tree. However, they disobeyed God and ate from the tree that God had commanded them not to. In their disobedience, all humanity died, just as God said they would. So man is no longer worthy of life but is now worthy of death. He is now disconnected from Almighty God and deserving of the second death: to be cast in the lake of fire along with Satan and his demons, to be eternally separated from God's presence. We are now dead men walking, not connected to our life source, God Almighty.

But that's not the end of this story because Jesus tells us in John 3:16 (KJV)

> *"For God so loved the world, that he gave his only begotten Son, that whosoever believeth in him should not perish, but have everlasting life".*

God's love for man is so great, and because he is created truly worthy [very good], man is now worthy through Jesus Christ of a second chance at eternal life. Here is the thing: Adam and his wife Eve took the forbidden fruit and ate it, but their children (descendants, you and I) didn't. We inherit the curse of the fall. Adam and Eve did not have children until after they disobeyed God which caused the fall from grace. In their sins, they passed down the nature of sin and the curse of the fall to their descendants. That is to say, it was passed down to us, mankind. Our God is a just God!

God sent his Son, Jesus, to die, pay the price for our

redemption, to redeem us back to God, that whosoever believes in Jesus, even in His Name, shall have everlasting life. God wants to reconcile us back to Himself. To make us truly worthy of life again, but it can only come through Jesus Christ, God's only begotten or unique Son. Jesus is the only one worthy to pay the price for our salvation and redemption for our sins, because He lived a life without committing any sin or evil. Jesus lived a perfect life that pleased God, and because of what He did, God the Father gave saving grace to everyone who believed in Jesus and confessed him as Lord and Savior. In 2 Corinthians 5:21, the word says,

> *"For he hath made him to be sin for us, who knew no sin; that we might be made the righteousness of God in him."*

We must obey and do the words and teachings of Jesus Christ. Because Jesus was the only one (that is man) to have lived a perfect life, God the Father has made Him the only one worthy to give life. Paul teaches us that we must present our bodies as a living sacrifice through Jesus Christ, to be holy and acceptable to God. Then Paul tells us, as Disciples of Christ Jesus, that we are to live our lives as prisoners of the Lord. This may sound strange, as though we are bound and in bondage as Christians, but we are not. The truth is that Christ has made us free, and being disciples, this is the way we should live our lives, and that we are to walk worthy of the vocation or calling given by God that He called you to do.

When you read and study Ephesians 4:1-32, your manner of communication ought to reflect the character of Christ, who spoke what was good and edifying to all, and did so in love. We are exhorted to let no corrupt word proceed from our mouths, but only that which is good for edification, that it may impart grace to the hearers. In all things, we are to act in love, doing good to all, for our words possess a power that mirrors, in some measure, the creative power of God's own Word. As the Scriptures record in Genesis 2:19-20, the Lord brought every beast of the field and every bird of the air to Adam, to see what he would call them; and whatever Adam called each living creature, that was its name. Thus, Adam exercised divinely delegated authority through his words, and what he spoke became reality. This took place before the fall.

In light of this, the apostle Paul admonishes us in Ephesians 4 to put off the old self, with its corrupt practices and speech, and to put on the new self, which is created after the likeness of God in true righteousness and holiness. As followers of Christ, we are called to speak and act in ways that are good, lovely, and of a good report, thereby walking worthy of the calling with which we have been called. By speaking the truth in love and manifesting the light of Christ within us to the world, we dispel darkness and draw others to the saving light of Jesus, our Savior. In so doing, we exemplify the grace of God in our lives, living in accordance with His Word and will, and walk as beloved children, pleasing Him by walking in love and doing all things for His glory.

Herein is our hope in the saving grace of God for all who believe in Christ: when we come to a true knowledge and understanding of "The Saving Grace of God" as it pertains to our lives. Our Lord Jesus Christ came to accomplish the will of His Father, who sent Him into the world. The will of the Father is to seek and to save that which was lost, and that of all whom the Father has given to Him, He should lose none, but raise them up at the last day, as declared in John 6:38-40.

According to the Scriptures, the lost are to respond to God's Word as set forth in Romans 10:9-10: by confessing with their mouth that Jesus is Lord, that He is the Son of God, who was crucified, died, was buried, and rose again on the third day, and by believing in their heart that God raised Jesus from the dead, they shall be saved. Upon salvation, the Holy Spirit baptizes the believer into the body of Christ, irrespective of race, gender, or nationality, as affirmed in 1 Corinthians 12:13. At this point, the Holy Spirit also seals the believer in the body of Christ until the day of redemption, in accordance with Ephesians 4:30.

It is incumbent upon us, as a sacred duty, to proclaim to the world the message of Jesus Christ, the gospel or good news, who is Himself "The Saving Grace of God", extended to all humanity. This responsibility compels us to bear witness to Christ, that all may know the redemptive grace offered through Him to the entire world. Should we fail to proclaim Christ to the world; the world will remain ignorant of His true identity and the divine purpose for which He was sent. Jesus Christ is the sole means by which humanity may come to the Heavenly Father; no one can approach the Father except through Him. For it is the Father Himself who draws individuals to Himself through His Son, Jesus Christ.

In the divine economy of grace, no distinction is drawn on the basis of one's identity, be it gender, race, color, nationality, or past deeds. In every circumstance,

Jesus Christ remains the all-sufficient answer. Should you be afflicted in body, He is the Great Physician who brings healing; if you are captive, He is the Deliverer who grants freedom. Whether your trials are physical, mental, spiritual, or financial, Christ alone is able to restore you to complete wholeness. There exists no problem or situation beyond the power of the Lord, for with Him, nothing is impossible. Christ is the Healer in the sickroom, the Advocate in the courtroom, and His grace is ever sufficient, as the Lord explained to the Apostle Paul in 2 Corinthians 12:9 when He said,

> *"And he said unto me, My **grace** is sufficient for thee: for my strength is made perfect in weakness..." (KJV)*

There is no transgression beyond His capacity to forgive. Regardless of your actions, your thoughts, or the circumstances you face, God's ultimate answer is revealed in His Son, Jesus Christ. If you are sick, He is your healer; if you are bound, He is your deliverer; if you are lost or dead, He is your savior; in every need, He is present to help. To receive God's saving grace, you have to accept Jesus Christ as your Lord and Savior because He is "The Saving Grace of God".

At the conclusion of this book, you will find a prayer for salvation. I earnestly exhort and entreat you to approach this prayer with a sincere heart and faith in its promise. Whatever your situation may be, Jesus Christ stands ready and willing to save all who call upon Him.

# CONCLUSION

𝒰ltimately, upon contemplation of the saving grace of God, it becomes evident that every individual is a recipient of His boundless grace, manifested in manifold ways throughout each day of our existence. While it is essential to possess a sound understanding of the nature of grace, it is of even greater importance to apprehend its surpassing significance and inestimable value for all humanity. From the moment we arise in the morning until we retire at night, we are sustained and encompassed by innumerable expressions of divine grace, often unrecognized and unacknowledged by those who receive them. My earnest prayer is that, through the study of this book, you have been enabled to perceive and appreciate, even the most seemingly insignificant, tokens of grace that have been lavishly bestowed upon you.

Let us ever bear in mind that, by its very definition, grace is unmerited favor: it is neither earned, nor deserved, nor owed, but is the free and sovereign manifestation of God's love toward humankind. As you traverse the course of each day, both in the quietness of the night and with the dawning of the morning, may you be moved to offer thanksgiving to God for the multitude of graces that He, as our Heavenly Father and through our Lord Jesus Christ, has graciously imparted. Let us also not lose sight of the fact that the saving grace of God is vital for all humanity. This grace is given to anyone who calls on the Name of the Lord and believes in the only begotten Son of God, the Lord Jesus Christ. The saving grace of God is necessary for everyone who desires eternal life through Christ Jesus, and without this grace, no one can be saved. Among the various kinds and manifold expressions of grace, there is yet one that stands supreme, the saving grace of God, which is preeminent, above all others.

This saving grace is the gracious gift of God the Father, procured through the redemptive work of His only begotten Son upon the cross. In the fullness of time, God sent forth Jesus Christ to redeem humanity, offering Himself as the atoning sacrifice for our sins through His crucifixion. Upon that cross, He bore the penalty of our iniquities, and thus, it is incumbent upon us to confess with our mouths the Lord Jesus and to believe in our hearts that God has raised Him from the dead, for in so doing, Scripture assures us, we shall be saved.

Thus, it is by Grace that we are saved, through faith, and this Grace is itself the gift of God, not the result of human effort, lest any should boast. This Grace delivers us from the coming wrath of God reserved for Satan, his demons, and the children of disobedience. Therefore, let us not be found among the disobedient, but rather let us walk in obedience to the Word of God, placing our faith wholly in the Lord Jesus Christ.

Furthermore, it is imperative that we seek to know ourselves in light of God's purpose for our lives. Seek the Lord while He may be found, for now is the acceptable time, and today is the day of salvation. In seeking Him and submitting to His will, He will supply all your needs, serve as your protector and guide, and lead you in the path of righteousness. He will be your strength, your shield, and your defender. Above all, He will be your grace and your salvation. Truly, as children of God, we are supremely blessed, to be saved by the grace of God through our faith in Christ Jesus.

The grace of God is His unmerited and sovereign gift to humanity, bestowed upon all who place their faith in the only begotten Son of God. It is through believing that God, in His infinite mercy, sent His Son, Jesus Christ, to offer Himself as a ransom for many, thereby redeeming humanity unto God, our Heavenly Father. Every individual who approaches God must do so in the conviction that Jesus is the Savior of the world, the Son sent by the Father for the express purpose of delivering mankind from the bondage of sin. Such faith requires assent to the saving work of Christ: His atoning death by crucifixion, His burial, and His resurrection on the third day. Moreover, genuine faith is evidenced by embracing and living according to His teachings, the Gospel, which proclaims the good news of the Kingdom of Heaven and affirms that Christ came forth from the Father to accomplish the redemption of the world.

Grace constitutes the unbreakable bond of God's salvific purpose for our souls, accomplished through the atoning sacrifice of His Son, Jesus Christ, the living God who now dwells within believers. In those moments when the presence of grace evokes joy in our hearts, or moves us to tears in the light of its profound meaning, we bear witness to the manifold testimonies of God's love. Acts of compassion, forgiveness, and benevolence, when offered freely and generously, often in defiance of worldly expectations, embody the very essence of grace in our lives. When we look at the different ways people can experience grace, we find that its heart lies in qualities like compassion, forgiveness, and kindness. Grace stands apart from the idea that rewards always come from effort or merit. Instead, it shows up in many forms, such as mercy, pardon, favor, and charity, and there are even more ways it can be seen. Sometimes, we notice preserving grace when

God helps someone overcome challenges, even those as serious as death. Other examples include kindness we do not deserve, forgiveness, and the grace that comes from waiting patiently for God's blessings. Grace can also mean protection, provision, and deliverance. While all forms of grace are significant, the saving grace of God is considered the most important, as it provides salvation and eternal life. This grace allows people to escape the second death, which is the coming judgment for those who reject Jesus Christ, the Son of God.

All forms of grace come from God through Jesus Christ. When others show us grace, it is because God wills it, not because we deserve it. Grace reaches us through Jesus Christ, God Son because Adam's disobedience brought the curse of the fall. In response to this, Jesus came as our deliverer, redeemer, Savior, and the Son of God. God sent his Son not to condemn the world for its sin, but so that the world could be saved through him. This is how we receive grace through Jesus Christ.

The saving grace of God is a gift that neither can be purchased nor is ever deserved; yet, in His boundless mercy, God the Father freely extends this grace to all who believe by faith in His only begotten Son. Such grace is not extended to non-believers until they come to know the truth of God through faith in Jesus Christ and accept Him as Lord and Savior. Though by our fallen nature we are subject to the second death, to be cast into the lake of fire prepared for Satan and his fallen angels, God, in His great love, has delivered us from such a fate.

Having now considered the meaning of grace, the person and work of Jesus Christ, and the means by which one receives God's saving grace, it is fitting to recall the fundamental importance of grace in the divine economy. Why is grace so vital and why is it so desperately needed? After the tragic fall of man in the Garden of Eden, owing to the disobedience of Adam and Eve, God, in His unfathomable love, ordained a redemptive plan to reconcile humanity to himself.

This plan of salvation would be accomplished through His only begotten Son, Jesus Christ, the eternal Word made flesh, thus fulfilling prophecy and bringing redemption to all peoples. In the fullness of time, God, in accordance with His sovereign will, caused a virgin to conceive and bear her firstborn Son, who is the Son of God and the Savior of the world.

Satan, together with all the angels who willfully believed and followed him in his rebellion, set themselves in opposition to Almighty God. Consequently, God, in His divine justice, has prepared the lake of fire as the place of their eternal punishment, for they are spirit beings, immortal and imperishable, and thus their judgment endures throughout all eternity. This place, ordained for the everlasting retribution of rebellious spirits, stands as a testament to the seriousness of their transgression.

Even though Adam disobeyed God in the Garden of Eden and humanity became separated from Him, God's love for us remained strong. He gave us His greatest gift: saving grace through His Son, Jesus Christ. Jesus came so that anyone who believes in Him will not perish but have eternal life. Through His sacrifice on the cross, Jesus shed His blood to wash away our sins and make us right with God. All anyone has to do to become a Child of God is what Romans 10:9-10 says,

> *"that if thou shalt confess with thy mouth the Lord Jesus, and shalt believe in thine heart that God hath raised him from the dead, thou shalt be saved. For with the heart man believeth unto righteousness; and with the mouth confession is made unto salvation."* *(King James Version)*

Also, in John 1:12 the Word reads'

> *"But as many as received him, to them gave he power to become the sons of God, even to them that believe on his name:"* *(KJV)*.

And in Galatians 3:26, the Word tells us that,

> *"For ye are all the children of God by faith in Christ Jesus."* *(KJV)*

Turning to humanity, although Adam and his wife Eve, by the exercise of their own free will, partook of the fruit of the tree of the knowledge of good and evil, we, their descendants, did not commit this initial act. The Scriptures testify that Eve was deceived, whereas Adam acted with full knowledge. As it is written in 1 Timothy 2:13-15 (KJV):

> *"For Adam was first formed, then Eve. And Adam was not deceived, but the woman being deceived was in the transgression. Notwithstanding she shall be saved in childbearing, if they continue in faith and charity and holiness with sobriety."*

Although by reason of Adam's disobedience, all humanity stands worthy of death but God, in His infinite love for the world, for mankind, who He created in His image and after His likeness, and pronounced "very good", has graciously granted man a second opportunity for eternal life. He extends this grace, not on the basis of works, lest any should boast, but through faith in His only begotten Son, so that all who believes may receive the promise of salvation through Him.

It is by faith that one receives the grace of God: when a person confesses with their mouth the Lord Jesus and believes in their heart that God has raised Him from the dead, salvation is assured. As the Apostle Paul affirms, referencing the words of the Lord to Moses in Romans 9:15 (KJV):

> *"For he saith to Moses, I will have mercy on whom I will have mercy, and I will have compassion on whom I will have compassion."*

This declaration finds its origin in Exodus 33:19 (KJV):

> *"And he said, I will make all my goodness pass before thee, and I will proclaim the name of the LORD before thee; and will be gracious to whom I will be gracious, and will shew mercy on whom I will shew mercy."*

Therefore, Jesus came from God the Father in Heaven because he was sent to seek and save those who are lost. God sent His Son to save man from their sins and to redeem mankind to God, because man was created in

God's image and likeness. Man is the apple of God's eye, created to be like the Lord, and God gave Adam dominion over the works of His hand on earth. But because of the fall in the Garden of Eden, Adam sinned and became lost, separated from God. So God sent his son to redeem mankind and to die for all humanity.

Whoever believes in the Lord Jesus can receive the gift of saving grace through Jesus Christ and have eternal life. This was Jesus' purpose for coming into the world, sent by God the Father. Jesus is God's only begotten Son who became flesh, a man like us, who was with the Father before the foundation of the world. This unique Son is the Word of God made flesh. God the Father prepared a body for His Word, which became flesh and His unique Son, sent into the world to redeem mankind to Himself. Therefore, Jesus Christ, the unique Son of God, is the *Saving Grace of God. The* Word of God tells us we are saved by grace through faith. This makes Jesus our saving grace, who died on the cross so we may have everlasting life. Glory be to God!

Now, as we conclude this book, remember that the answer to how a person receives God's saving grace is simple. Just as the Trinity, Father, Son, and Holy Spirit, worked together in creating the universe, all three are at work in the rebirth of a person. Those who accept Jesus as the Son of God and believe in their heart that God raised him from the dead are granted the gift of salvation by God the Father. Why does this happen and how? It is because of what Jesus did on the cross, His teachings about the Kingdom of Heaven, and the gospel (the good news), and those who believe can receive God's free gift.

Jesus explained who he was and his purpose for coming. Those who believe and accept Jesus Christ as the Son of God are blessed by the Heavenly Father when we do what Romans 10:9-10 says: confess with our mouth the Lord Jesus Christ, that he is the Son of God, that he was crucified, died, was buried, and on the third day, God raised him from the dead. We then acknowledge that we are sinners, have sinned against God, and need a savior, confessing and believing that the savior is Jesus the Christ. When we act on these words by confessing with our mouth and believing in our heart Jesus is the Son of God He grants us the gift of salvation.

This gift is something we do not deserve, cannot earn, and cannot afford. It is given freely by God Almighty because of our faith in Jesus Christ. When this happens, as new believers, we are baptized by the Holy Spirit into the Body of Christ. We are born again of the Spirit of God, meaning our spirit is regenerated and transformed as we renew our mind to be like Christ, who is the word of God. As a result, we strive to do what is holy, righteous, and pleasing to God.

It was God's intention for Adam to be like Him at the beginning of creation. But Adam and Eve disobeyed God and fell in the garden, becoming separated from Him. Because of their separation from the Lord, all humanity is dead to God until we are born again of the Spirit of God. After the Holy Spirit baptizes us into the Body of Christ, he seals us in Christ's Body. In this way, what Jesus said is fulfilled: he would not lose any that the Father has given him.

We see the saving grace of God in the gift of eternal

life that comes through Jesus Christ, our Lord. The Father, Son, and Holy Spirit not only worked together at the creation of man, but also continue to work together through the rebirth of those who are born again of God's Spirit, those who accept Jesus Christ as Lord and Savior.

Here is the important question: How can someone receive God's saving grace? I am glad to share the answer from the Bible. This saving *grace* is salvation, which gives eternal life and the power to become a child of God. According to Romans 10:9-10, anyone who confesses with their mouth that Jesus is Lord and believes in their heart that God raised him from the dead will be saved. Believing in your heart leads to righteousness, and speaking your faith leads to salvation. Thus, the dispensation of grace and mercy rests solely upon the sovereign will of God, who acts in accordance with His perfect will, wisdom and love. **Amen! Hallelujah!**

# PRAYER OF THANKSGIVING

Heavenly Father in Jesus' holy name, I give you thanks, glory, honor, and praise for all you have done, are doing, and will do. God and Father of our Lord Jesus, thank you for your mercy, love, and kindness, and for being my strength, strong tower, and refuge. Thank you for the love in my heart and for being my fortress, shield, and protector. I place my trust in you to lead, guide, and deliver me. Lord, you are my God, my savior, and my salvation.

Heavenly Father these are my requests: First, I pray for everyone around the world, asking that you touch their hearts, transform their lives, and open their minds to the truth of your Word. May people everywhere come to know and understand your truth that is your Word. Please grant them wisdom, knowledge, understanding, revelation, and illumination. Order our steps in your Word, lead us in the path of righteousness, and help us to become who you created us to be.

I also pray that your will be done on Earth as it is in Heaven. Most of all, I thank you for your saving grace, the gift of salvation through faith in Jesus Christ. Thank you for this grace. I pray all this in Jesus' Holy Name. Amen.
.

# PRAYER FOR SALVATION

*J*f you do not know Jesus Christ and have not accepted Him as your Lord and Savior, or if you are a backslider who went back into world but you want to come back to Him, I would like to help by leading you in a prayer for salvation.

The scriptures tell us in Romans Chapter 10, Verses 9 and 10,

> *"that if you confess with your mouth the Lord Jesus and believe in your heart that God has raised Him from the dead, you will be saved. For with the heart one believes unto righteousness, and with the mouth confession is made unto salvation." (NKJV)*

And 1 John 1:9 says,

> *"If we confess our sins, he is faithful and just to forgive us our sins, and to cleanse us from all unrighteousness." (KJV)*

So, if you will just repeat aloud these words and say

> ***Heavenly Father, I believe Jesus is Your Son and that You sent Him to save me. I believe He died on the cross, shed His blood, and rose from the dead on the third day. Lord Jesus, please forgive me of my sins and come live in my heart. Make me a new creation, and I accept You as my Lord and Savior. Thank You, Heavenly Father, for saving me in Jesus' Name I pray. Amen.***

If you read and believed this prayer, let me be the first to congratulate you. Welcome to the Body of Christ and the family of God. I rejoice with the holy angels in Heaven. Once again, welcome to the Body of Jesus Christ. You have now been Born Again!

To receive free information about your next steps as a Born Again Child of God, please send email to cthomasbooks@gmail.com with the subject line "Where do I go from here?" If you prefer to receive materials by mail, include your mailing address. Thank you for reading the book, and may you be blessed in Jesus' name. Amen!

# SUPPORTING SCRIPTURES TO READ

*"For I came down from heaven, not to do mine own will, but the will of him that sent me. And this is the Father's will which hath sent me, that of all which he hath given me I should lose nothing, but should raise it up again at the last day. And this is the will of him that sent me, that every one which seeth the Son, and believeth on him, may have everlasting life: and I will raise him up at the last day."* John 6:38-40 (KJV).

*"That if thou shalt confess with thy mouth the Lord Jesus, and shalt believe in thine heart that God hath raised him from the dead, thou shalt be saved. For with the heart man believeth unto righteousness; and with the mouth confession is made unto salvation."* Romans 10:9-10 (KJV)

*"For by one Spirit are we all baptized into one body, whether we be Jews or Gentiles, whether we be bond or free; and have been all made to drink into one Spirit."* 1 Corinthians 12:13 (KJV)

*"And grieve not the holy Spirit of God, whereby ye are sealed unto the day of redemption."* Ephesians 4:30 (KJV)

## How we are to conduct ourselves as believers and children of God

Ephesians 4:1-32, which reads,
*"I therefore, the prisoner of the Lord, beseech you that ye walk worthy of the vocation wherewith ye are called, with all lowliness and meekness, with longsuffering, forbearing one another in love; endeavouring to keep the unity of the*

*Spirit in the bond of peace. There is one body, and one Spirit, even as ye are called in one hope of your calling; one Lord, one faith, one baptism, one God and Father of all, who is above all, and through all, and in you all. But unto every one of us is given grace according to the measure of the gift of Christ. Wherefore he saith, When he ascended up on high, he led captivity captive, And gave gifts unto men. (Now that he ascended, what is it but that he also descended first into the lower parts of the earth? He that descended is the same also that ascended up far above all heavens, that he might fill all things.) And he gave some, apostles; and some, prophets; and some, evangelists; and some, pastors and teachers; for the perfecting of the saints, for the work of the ministry, for the edifying of the body of Christ: till we all come in the unity of the faith, and of the knowledge of the Son of God, unto a perfect man, unto the measure of the stature of the fulness of Christ: that we henceforth be no more children, tossed to and fro, and carried about with every wind of doctrine, by the sleight of men, and cunning craftiness, whereby they lie in wait to deceive; but speaking the truth in love, may grow up into him in all things, which is the head, even Christ: from whom the whole body fitly joined together and compacted by that which every joint supplieth, according to the effectual working in the measure of every part, maketh increase of the body unto the edifying of itself in love. This I say therefore, and testify in the Lord, that ye henceforth walk not as other Gentiles walk, in the vanity of their mind, having the understanding darkened, being alienated from the life of God through the ignorance that is in them, because of the blindness of their heart: who being past feeling have given themselves over unto lasciviousness, to work all uncleanness with greediness. But ye have not so learned Christ; if so be that ye have heard him, and have been taught by him, as the truth is in Jesus: that ye put off concerning the former conversation the old man, which is corrupt according to the deceitful lusts; and be renewed in the spirit of your mind; and that ye put on the new man, which after God is created in righteousness and true holiness. Wherefore putting away lying, speak every man truth with his neighbour: for we are members one of another. Be ye angry, and sin not: let not the sun go down upon your wrath: neither give place to the devil. Let him that stole steal no more: but rather let him labour, working with his hands the thing which is good, that he may have to give to him that needeth. Let no corrupt communication proceed out of your mouth, but that which is good to the use of edifying, that it may minister grace unto the hearers. And grieve not the holy Spirit of God, whereby ye are sealed unto the day of redemption. Let all bitterness, and wrath, and anger, and clamour, and evil speaking, be put away from you, with all malice: and be ye kind one to another, tenderhearted, forgiving one another, even as God for Christ's sake hath forgiven you."* (KJV).

# ABOUT THE AUTHOR

Minister Cheyenne Thomas is divinely called to the ministries of teaching, preaching, and pastoral leadership within the Body of Christ. Endowed with a passion for the edification of God's people, he has faithfully pursued the call to serve the Church in these capacities. In addition to his ministerial vocation, Cheyenne attained an Associate in Applied Science degree from the Borough of Manhattan Community College in New York City during the early 1980s. He also brings over eighteen years of professional experience in software development to his ministry, having acquired proficiency in multiple programming languages. Through the integration of his theological training and technical expertise, Cheyenne seeks to advance the cause of Christ and to equip the saints for effective service in both spiritual and practical domains. Minister Cheyenne is a husband and father. Cheyenne met and married his lovely wife, Joanne, in 1985, and from this union God blessed them with four wonderful children: three daughters and a son.

www.ingramcontent.com/pod-product-compliance
Lightning Source LLC
Chambersburg PA
CBHW021241090426
42740CB00006B/632